E N D O R S E M

RETURN TO ~~MILLBORO~~

"I have met Marge Rieder and a number of the people in her research and believe them all to be people of integrity. Their story cannot be explained away as fiction. Therefore it is undoubtedly one of the most significant accounts in print to date which presents verifiable facts pointing to previous lifetimes of individuals living today.

"For a full appreciation of her second book, the reader should be familiar with *Mission to Millboro*. *Return to Millboro* describes in fascinating detail the lives of all of the people introduced in the first book. One of the most interesting features of *Return to Millboro* is the detailed account of the historical Underground Railroad. Although at times the reader may have to concentrate to keep the characters, who all have two identities, separated, the author has facilitated this problem by giving each of them a separate chapter.

"Marge Rieder is to be highly complimented and deeply appreciated for the meticulous research she has done on this dramatic period of our history. Not only has she presented incontrovertible evidence of the reality of a pre-existence for all of us, but she has produced a detailed account of an important part of American history at that time."

—Hazel M. Denning, Ph.D.

"The entranced Edgar Cayce spoke of group reincarnation— Marge Rieder has demonstrated it. In this sequel to *Mission to Millboro,* she presents the conclusion of an air-tight case for group rebirth, proving it beyond a reasonable doubt. The evidence—both internal and external—is overwhelming. Under hypnosis, in a nine-year study, total strangers have revealed identical accounts of Civil War Millboro, Virginia, which are buttressed by substantial physical evidence, photographs, and government records, including a mind-boggling letter sent to Jefferson Davis . . . an extraordinary piece of past-life research, the best of its kind to date."

—George Schwimmer, Ph.D., author of *The Search for David*

Also by Marge Rieder
Mission to Millboro: A Study in Group Reincarnation
(Blue Dolphin, 1993)

More Endorsements for
Return to Millboro

"Marge Rieder has done it again! *Return to Millboro* is even more compelling reading than its predecessor as her cast of Civil War characters expands to include pre-historic Indians, runaway slaves and the underground railroad. Their stories, backed by meticulous on-site research, serve to remind us that for the Soul, yesterday's pains and pleasures underpin attitudes we're still struggling to reconcile today. Past-life therapy can help. I highly recommend this book."
—Chet B. Snow, Ph.D., author of *Mass Dreams of the Future*

"*Return to Millboro* is one of those 'I've got to sit down and read all the way to the end' kind of books. It is filled with detailed descriptions of past lives, augmented by photographs, historical documents, and other supportive data. One of the fascinations of doing past life therapy is being able to retrieve historically validated information."
—Russell C. Davis, Ph.D.

"The Millboro case is one of the most fascinating examples of group reincarnation I have ever read. After personally meeting three of the subjects, I am even more impressed with their story."
—Bruce Goldberg, D.D.S., M.S., author of
The Search for Grace and *Past Lives—Future Lives*

"Millboro's melodramatic Civil War past has been laid bare—a most remarkable case study strongly suggestive of reincarnation."
—A. Robert Smith, editor of *Venture Inward*

RETURN
TO
MILLBORO

THE
REINCARNATION DRAMA
CONTINUES . . .

MARGE RIEDER, Ph.D.

Foreword by A. Robert Smith

Blue Dolphin Publishing

Published by Blue Dolphin Publishing, Inc.
P.O. Box 8, Nevada City, CA 95959
Orders: 1-800-643-0765

ISBN: 0-931892-28-7

Library of Congress Cataloging-in-Publication Data

Rieder, Marge.
    Return to Millboro / Marge Rieder.
      p. cm.
    ISBN 0-931892-28-7 (paper)
    1. Reincarnation—California, Southern—Case studies.
  2. Millboro (Va.)—History—19th century—Miscellanea.
  3. Millboro (Va.)—Biography—Miscellanea.   I. Title.
    BF1156.R45R55   1995
    133.9'01'3—dc20   95-41447
                                     CIP

Printed in the United States of America by
Blue Dolphin Press, Inc., Grass Valley, California

5   4   3   2   1

. . . and so it seems that we have met before,
and laughed before and loved before,
but who knows where or when?

"Where or When," from the musical
Babes in Arms (1926), by Rogers and Hart

DEDICATION

This book is dedicated to the memory of
Barbara Jean Roberts, who portrayed both
Liz and Singing Bird,
and Robin Park, who portrayed Warm Sun
in *Mission to Millboro.*

FLY FREE, SUN BIRD, SOAR HIGH,
UP OVER THE ROBIN'S NEST!

ACKNOWLEDGMENTS

Among the many persons who contributed and assisted in this research, I would like to give special thanks to the following: My lifelong friend, Bill Hampton, for outstanding work on the photos; Hot Springs Realtor Larry Fresh, for his help in locating property owners in the Millboro area; Mr. Harry Jolly of Burlington, North Carolina, whose mother was a Bratton—Mr. Jolly has provided me with documented insight into the colorful history of Millboro; Mr. Jodey Bateman of Silver City, New Mexico, for helpful insight into the history of East Coast Indians; Mr. James Croy of Warm Springs, Virginia, for supplying old documents; to Charley Williams, owner of the property where "Grandma's house" stood, for making it possible to get pictures of the hidden room on that property; and lastly, to Mr. Heilman in Millboro, for making available old books and documents regarding the Millboro area.

TABLE OF CONTENTS

FOREWORD

WHEN ANYONE REMEMBERS FRAGMENTS of another life in an earlier time, as do the many people who inhabit this fascinating tale of Civil War Millboro, Virginia, I have a strong impulse to pull on my deerstalker and go play Sherlock Holmes, investigating the locale, searching for clues, piecing together bits and pieces of evidence to verify this person's memory and, possibly, even discover the perfect case. The perfect case of a past-life memory, of course, would prove once and for all the validity of the theory of reincarnation.

I am only one of many investigators with this unquenchable thirst for the truth of this idea that our souls survive one bodily death only to reappear in another body and take on another persona, and perhaps another and another down through the centuries, as Edgar Cayce, the Theosophists, and others maintained.

Somehow, however, the perfect case eludes us. Ian Stevenson, the world-famous author-psychiatrist and reincarnation researcher, has compiled some 2500 cases in a lifetime of field research in the Orient, the Middle East, and even the Arctic. In his careful, scientific approach, Dr. Stevenson gains credibility--but is cautious to say that his cases are "suggestive" of reincarnation, but not necessarily proof positive.

K.S. Rawat, director of the Reincarnation Research Foundation in India, is also looking for the perfect case. And his country seems to offer more cases than any other on earth, possibly because the concept of reincarnation is familiar and more widely accepted there than in the West, where prevailing Christian doctrine resists reincarnation as an alien belief.

In a recent issue of my magazine, *Venture Inward,* Dr. Rawat and Dr. Stevenson confessed to one another that they are still searching for an ideal case. Usually, something is missing, or a memory doesn't check out with known historical records, or the subject describes people of another time and place that defy the best detective work in the search for verification. "I would like to find better cases," Stevenson remarked. "However, the ideal or perfect case, I don't think we will ever find. I don't know if such cases really exist, but we are always trying . . ."

The Millboro story pieced together by Marge Rieder, in her work as a hypnotherapist, and recounted first in *Mission to Millboro,* and now in this sequel, also has missing pieces. It would not, I think, merit being called a perfect case. And yet it is powerfully persuasive to me. Certainly it is endlessly fascinating in its utter uniqueness--a large group of people with past-life memories of having once lived in a town which none of them in this life had ever heard of or set foot in.

Moreover, the Millboro story doesn't depend entirely on how Rieder's subjects describe it for us. Millboro, or what is left of it, still stands. We can visit the place and see for ourselves what they were talking about on Rieder's therapeutic couch. I visited this quaint village in the Blue Ridge Mountains myself, spending a day there with Marge Rieder and two principal figures in this story, Maureen Williamson, who was Becky in Millboro, and Maureen's husband, Ralph "Smokey" Williamson, who was a Yankee sympathizer and printer named Samuel who had a fling with Becky. I spent that day as much to evaluate them as the town, and I came away persuaded of their guileless sincerity in searching for their roots. They, too, were on a quest for truth.

The Millboro story is doubly engrossing because it involved so many people who are once again living in fairly close proximity to one another. Is there an explanation for this? Rieder offers none, except that they may have all been drawn to sulphur springs, which are plentiful around Millboro and once were abundant in the Palm

Springs area where many of Rieder's subjects lived. Edgar Cayce suggests another explanation: people "are grouped as associates again because of an urge of a complex or compound nature, or because of a universal urge." Many of Cayce's followers believe they once were together in ancient Egypt, when he was thought to have been a high priest and their spiritual leader. A large contingent of them today live in Virginia Beach, Virginia, headquarters of the Cayce Foundation. Group reincarnation, in a word, is simply a case of souls following their urges to hang out with familiar souls.

My conclusion about the Millboro mystery is as intuitive as evidential: if Millboro is a picture puzzle in which some pieces are missing or out of place, a vivid, dramatic picture of this town, caught in the passions of war and romance, comes through from all the many pieces that the author has put in place. One creative person might have pulled such a compelling scenario from his or her imagination. But a couple of dozen people? Not likely.

I believe that Millboro's past has been laid bare. And it will stand as a most remarkable case study very suggestive of reincarnation, until someone proves otherwise.

Read the story, visit the town, and draw your own conclusions.

A. Robert Smith
Editor, *Venture Inward*

Maureen Williamson (Becky), Marge Rieder (author),
and Joe Nazarowski (Charley) appear
on the Larry King Show *in September, 1993.*

INTRODUCTION

RETURN TO MILLBORO reveals many more aspects of the amazingly interwoven lives that were recounted in a previous volume, *Mission to Millboro* (Blue Dolphin, 1993). The following is a brief synopsis of the story and characters, as presented in *Mission to Millboro.*

After a business meeting with several local law enforcement officers, Maureen Williamson went with a group to a restaurant, where she ordered carrot cake. This surprised her because, according to Maureen, she has no great fondness for carrot cake. It was this incident, she claims, that triggered the memory of Becky, who lived long ago in the small Virginia town of Millboro. Becky's husband, John, had been a lawman who loved carrot cake.

Under hypnosis, she has told us the story of Becky's life and exposed the fact that a great many of Maureen's friends and acquaintances today—Barbara, Joe, Millie, and others—lived lives back in Millboro along with Becky.

The story started when Liz (John's mother and Barbara Roberts today) was born in the early 1800s to an Indian mother and an Irish father. Shortly after puberty, she married a man named Ailstock and moved to Bath County to the area of Green Valley, near Millboro. After being widowed, she met and fell deeply in love with a young Indian brave known as Little Eagle and moved to the Indian village of Robin's Nest, high in the hills above Millboro, where they were married in an Indian ceremony. When their son,

John, was about four years old, she was ordered by the Indian council to move into town so he could attend the white man's school. Neither Liz nor her son looked Indian.

John grew up to become the lawman in Millboro, and at about age twenty he married Becky Cunningham, who claims to be from Herndon, Virginia. They set up housekeeping on the edge of town and had several children: Phoebe, Robert, Rachel, Elizabeth, and baby Peter. Becky's best friend in town was a girl named Constance; they spent many hours together and managed to get into and out of trouble with very little effort.

Shortly after the Civil War started, Charley Morgan (Joe Nazarowski today) came to town. He was a Confederate soldier who had been wounded at Shiloh and who moved to Millboro ostensibly to train horses for the Confederacy. We discovered, while researching *Mission to Millboro,* that Charley was in reality a Confederate spy sent to town to blow up the railroad tunnel, should the Yanks invade the town.

Because John was head of the Union spy ring in Millboro, he was gone almost constantly, and Becky, not one to endure loneliness for very long, turned for comfort to Charley. She had had an affair previously with Samuel (Ralph Williamson today), a journalist who came to town regularly. Their affair had ended abruptly and mysteriously when Becky became pregnant, by Samuel, with baby Peter.

Charley stayed in the town boarding house, which was owned and operated by Honey, a charming and popular woman, who today is Millie Sproule.

Ruthie (Jackie Spagnolo today) was a cousin of Constance's who came to live with Constance's family when she was orphaned. Because of Constance's obsessive jealously of her very pretty cousin, Ruthie went to live out in the country in an old plantation house with an elderly couple, who raised her as their own. After the war started, she left their estate and took up residence in the whorehouse in Millboro, until she was accidentally shot and killed a few years later.

When Sharon Olive (Elizabeth of Green Valley Farm) came from Texas to be hypnotized, she described how she had come to live in the old plantation house in Green Valley after Ruthie left. She was sent there because her family thought she would be safer away from the main battlegrounds of the war, but also she was there to assist the old man, who was virtually alone, because his wife had died earlier in the war. He had sent most of his Negroes North to fight for the Union cause, and he really needed help in running the place. Sharon was the first to describe the hidden room (or rooms) in the basement, which had been used to conceal both escaped slaves and lost or escaped Union soldiers. They were concealed in hidden rooms in the basement, then smuggled out through a tunnel leading to the creek behind the house, then spirited, under cover of darkness and in flat-bottomed boats, down the creek behind the house, to awaiting wagons.

Because Becky was deeply involved in a love affair with Charley, Union Intelligence officials decided, unbeknownst to her husband John, that she was a threat to the entire spy ring, and they ordered her death. On January 20, 1865, Becky was raped and strangled by Jake Bauer, a drifter and ne'er-do-well. Elizabeth, Becky's youngest daughter, was hiding in the loft of the barn and watched, horror-stricken, as her mother was killed.

Becky's death had a devastating effect on her immediate family and on the town in general. Despite her reputation for promiscuity, Becky was a pretty, happy-go-lucky, effervescent girl, who was friendly as a puppy and well-loved by all who knew her.

Over the next couple of years, John found homes for his and Becky's children, placing Peter with Honey. When the typhoid epidemic, which had devastated the area immediately after the war, was finally under control and his children placed in good and loving homes, John left to reclaim his Indian roots, eventually settling with the Sioux tribe in "the Dakotas." And now, the saga continues. . . .

RUNNING SPRINGS
by Evie Rieder

For everything
is lost to the past.
I can't let go,
but I can't get back
to where I was before
I lost my heart.

The lines on my face
don't disappear
when I straighten up.
It's so unclear
where to go
when the signs are all torn down.

I've loved so many people
without knowing their names.
I've embraced mankind
and all its foolish games.
I've changed lead to gold
to find it's all the same,
and the rebel in me still yells
for release.

Solutions are crumpled up
on the floor,
using too much energy
trying to score . . .
all the things we think we need
to survive.

I have illusions,
I hide them with pain.
I've no solutions
and I've no refrain.
I have intrusions
into my brain;
they drive me crazy,
but I'm not insane.

I know things
that other people
don't.

Evie Rieder was born in Miami Beach, Florida.
Her profession is that of tool maker.
When she was three years old, her family lived in
Norfolk, Virginia, for two years.
Her father was a career Marine officer stationed there.
She has never been to Millboro.
She surfaces twice in the story of Millboro,
once as Roy Farmer, who owned a dairy farm near Millboro,
and also in another, earlier role, as Running Springs,
an Indian among the Robin's Nest tribes.

CHAPTER ONE

RUNNING SPRINGS

DURING THE TIME I WAS RESEARCHING *Mission to Millboro,* I discussed many aspects of the story with my daughter Evie, and on several occasions she insisted that she was part of this story.

Finally I hypnotized her and instructed her to regress to the time of the American Civil War. She was unable to see herself in or around Millboro. My conclusion was that she had heard me talk about this story so much that her imagination had told her she was a part of it.

At a later time, I hypnotized her for a totally unrelated reason. My instruction was, "Regress back into a lifetime in which you were very happy, contented, and fulfilled."

Immediately she started talking about a man named Roy. Roy was a dairy farmer who lived just outside of Williamsville, Virginia, about ten miles due north of Millboro. Roy died *just prior* to the advent of the Civil War. This emphasized to me how extremely literal the unconscious mind is. Had I instructed her to locate a lifetime *around* the time of the Civil War, she would undoubtedly have led me to Roy. We will meet and study Roy's life later in this narrative.

After we unearthed Roy, Evie informed me that she felt certain there was another, earlier lifetime buried in her mind, one that also related to the Millboro story.

She then introduced herself as Running Springs, saying, "I have the wisdom of the ages. I told the people this would befall them:

the white man would come, and we would have nothing left—nothing!"

The extremely gregarious Running Springs explained that she had always lived in the area of Robin's Nest. Her first exposure to white men happened when she was young, around age eleven or twelve. At that time, the country had very few white men, and they were not located in her vicinity. She had heard about them; then one day, there appeared a canoe on the river, and in it was one of the light skins. He was a trapper who had a long thing, a "noise stick" that frightened her. Later she claimed it was a musket. She was curious about the stranger but kept her distance.

Running Springs' father had once been the chief, but both her parents had died from the fever when she was very little, and she had become a "child of the tribe, grew up associating with all members of the tribe, and was everybody's child." Her early years, until about age twelve, were spent near the river, where Millboro Springs is today. Then, as the white man came in larger numbers and built the mill, the Indian group moved their village over to where the town of Millboro stands today. When the railroad came through the area, it presented a shock to the Indians and pretty much finished life as they had known it. They did everything they could to sabotage the railroad as it was being built. "We would steal the wooden ties and separate the tracks with large, strong sticks, and leave crossed skulls and artifacts on the site to intimidate the white man into thinking this was sacred burial ground. The tunnel was part way there (already), and the white men dug it on through the hill. That area was (in fact) a sacred Indian ceremonial ground; brave initiation ceremonies were held there, and up on the hill was a burial site." This fact has been verified by a member of the present-day Ailstock family, who informed me that she once owned 200 acres on Tunnel Hill in Millboro, which held many Indian burial mounds.

This was a time when the American government was concentrating on herding the large bulk of surviving Indians onto reservations. The Native Americans in the area of what was to become Millboro resisted and hid out, but, following the invasion of the railroad, white men came in such large numbers that the Indians were forced to retreat up the hill to the Robin's Nest area. "These arrogant white people came in here and decided it's their land!" Running Springs made no effort to conceal her bitterness. "We have been here thousands and thousands of years. My grandmother was born here; she saw the formation of the stars, the hills."

The earliest white men were very friendly and got along well with the Indians. "We taught them how to plant and to sow. They traded us tools and taught us some white man's ways." She was especially impressed with a tool given to the Indians called a "shovel."

Her clothing was generally a leather, sheath-type dress, with beads and pretty things sewn on the front. For the most part, she went barefoot, but in cold weather she wore skin boots that came up to above her ankles. The braves were good warriors but did little fighting, as theirs was an extremely peaceful tribe. This fact has been reiterated time and time again throughout this story, by both Indians and whites. The group was very intelligent and advanced, and they shared their talents and knowledge with other tribes in the area. A great deal of time was devoted to the tribal philosophy, *In-qua-da-day* (a search for meaning).

The warriors were excellent hunters who brought home wild turkeys and chicken, rabbits, deer, elk, and lots of fish. "There were no large animals such as buffalo." When I suggested bears, she replied facetiously, "Yeah, you gonna kill a bear with a bow and arrow?"

The women used the land well; they cultivated the land, while the men hunted; they grew maize (corn) and many grains and vegetables.

It was difficult to pin down Running Springs as to when she had lived exactly because she claimed that her spirit lived on long after her death and that she was aware of all that had transpired since her demise. Finally, together, we decided she had lived in the 1600s sometime, when white men first infiltrated Virginia.

Obviously, the gregarious old woman lived to a ripe old age, because during one of our earlier conversations she claimed to be very old and complained of tooth problems. "I need some soothing goat's milk for my teeth. Sometimes I rub oil on my gums and it helps." Despite her advanced age, she was very strong but had trouble getting around. Someone had made for her a litter-type carrier, "like the white man uses to carry off his dead." She would sit on it and be hauled about.

The tribe had a specific area for toilet facilities. "We walk in and we squat; then we cover it up." They bathed in the river, or "gorge," as she insisted upon calling it, and she had no idea what "soap" was. Whenever possible they would bathe in the warm sulfur, or "stinky" water, and Running Springs said she drank it every day. "It keeps you vital, keeps your system open, too. This is why the Indians here live so long, because of the water." Running Springs rhapsodized endlessly about the virtues of the sulfur water. "A very spiritual water; we use it in our religious ceremonies. It also rejuvenates when one is tired and contributes a lot to the success of our crops."

Though she was orphaned at a tender age, Running Springs had been well cared for by the tribe. Her father had been a much loved chief, and, when she was about twelve years of age, they realized she was special. She could accurately predict the weather, seemed to know when trouble was brewing, and, better yet, knew how best to handle it. She worked with the medicine man, and her skills as a healer were respected and sought out. Prior to giving readings or conducting a healing, Running Springs went through a purification process. She fasted, drank a black tea that made her vomit, and spent time alone in the woods until her spirit was properly attuned. Mostly though, she prided herself as the tribal storyteller and worked endlessly with the tribal children. Although she never married, she adored the little ones and patiently watched over them and taught them all she could.

As the regressions with Running Springs continued, we both came to realize that what we were dealing with was more than a past-life regression. What was happening was that Running Springs was being channeled. Her spirit has been "locked" in the Robin's Nest area for approximately 300 years, and she is impatiently waiting to be freed. Her first announcement to this effect was, "Find me, find me! I will be in the graveyard near the big, white rock. Send this one (Evie) to find me!!"

Running Springs made it abundantly clear that she did not particularly like me. One evening in Los Angeles, in front of many spectators, she turned toward me and stated clearly, *"Ka-pookey-pus!"* Then she translated, "You are very annoying. I wait and wait, and you ask these dumb questions. I have told you before; I was the storyteller of the tribe. I have been there for centuries in Robin's Nest. I am waiting in the burial grounds near the white rock. I will take you there; *bring Evie back!"*

Flabbergasted, I weakly explained that it all takes money and planning, and heard, *"Walk!* We Indians walk everywhere. Take a horse!"

While researching *Mission to Millboro,* there had transpired a session with Liz (Barbara Roberts), Becky (Maureen Williamson), and Honey (Millie Sproule). Out of a clear blue sky, Liz (who was married to an Indian) started describing a large, white rock in Robin's Nest. With tears running down her face, she verbally pictured a meadow with a very large, pristine, white rock in the center. Later she candidly explained that those were tears of rapture and joy. Evidently, to the Indians of Robin's Nest, that rock had a great religious significance, and many ceremonies were held under it. During the course of this study, that large, white rock has been mentioned many times, primarily by Indians, but recently Lila (Jan Dunwoody) drew me a map of its location. Consequently, it was no surprise when Running Springs started talking about the big, white rock. "It rises from the ground, higher than a man. Once it was freestanding, but now it is overgrown. The whiteness has diminished through the years; today it has a greyish hue. Our burial ground is behind it, near the bushes."

At an earlier time, Lenette Brychel, who regressed into a lifetime as a young girl named Sally in Civil War Millboro, had described a hidden room under her grandma's house, which was used to hide escaping slaves. It was Running Springs who told me that there were several such rooms under Millboro and that they had been built centuries earlier by the Indians.

Running Springs discussed the hidden, underground rooms at great length. In fact, she discussed everything at such great length and was so gregarious that we later decided her name should have been Running Mouth. "Many years ago, the Great Master told us that it would be necessary to build those rooms. The dome concept came from the Great Master; it was something he learned when he went back into the woods and spoke to the Power, the Source. He came back with the plans, and we didn't doubt him."

One day Maureen, who was reading a book concerning Native American tradition, called and asked if I had ever heard of a *kiva*. I had not. A *kiva*, I learned, is an underground room built by Native Americans, primarily in which to conduct religious ceremonies. Kivas are thought to be endemic principally to Pueblo Indians in North America. Upon hearing this, I called Evie and tranced her over the phone. When asked what a kiva was, to my amazement she answered, "It's a three-cornered tool . . . no, wait, a kiva is an underground room. The three-cornered tool is one of the things used to dig out and build a kiva."

Continuing, she explained that the rooms also had other names. One was a *Dug.* The actual kivas were used mostly for ceremonial meetings, which were limited exclusively to the older and more powerful men of the tribe. "Each one sat on his own rug, and they smoked wacky-weed, got stoned, made policy, and settled the tribe's problems."

Some of the rooms were used for other things, such as storing food. "Sometimes, in the cold months, we couldn't get food; the women had saved the dried food and locked it in some special kivas. We lived with the earth and the earth with us, in harmony—*Kam-pa-to* (living in harmony).

Once or twice in her life, there had been strong winds that caused much damage and knocked the village down. The entire tribe hid out in the underground rooms until the winds subsided. She stated that, in addition to ceremonial and storage caves, some of the men used the rooms for illicit reasons by bringing women into them.

It took the Indians many moons and the labor of many men to complete all the underground rooms. Everyone worked at it; even the children helped haul dirt out in bags and baskets. They dumped a lot of it in the woods, and some they hauled over to the river, or gorge, as she called it.

The stuff on the walls is a green concrete. The water they used (which contained sulfur) caused it to turn a greenish color. The concrete was made from crushed stone (probably river rock), a poisonous berry of some type found way out in the forest, and a tough, fibrous grass chopped very finely. This concoction was mixed using sticks, in a pail made from dried, hardened skin. The mixture was placed against the dirt wall by hand. "You have to wet your hands and put on leather gloves made from rabbit skin. We smear it and smooth it; then you have to get a new pair, because those would harden. We kept it wet while we were doing it, and we mixed grass and hay to make it pliable. When it hardens, you pull off the hay, and it's like good, solid rock. Hundreds of men worked over the years on those rooms; we had a lot of people come and go. The large holes were dug with sharpened limestone and sharp bones. The heavy, beamed ceilings were made from trees they had felled and planed themselves, hand hewn, handmade. We carved the wood by hand; then we treated it with a white, resin-like material, a paste we made of bone, the stinky water, sap from trees, and the juice of a root. The mixture smells very bad and is very toxic; several of the warriors became sick from the fumes, but it really seals. When the white man would come through, we would just take down our camp and go into the rooms. We would hide, and the white man would leave, saying that there's nothing here." This last revelation may explain how these particular Indians avoided being banished onto reservations long before they were.

During the course of these conversations and subsequent research regarding the underground rooms, I located a book entitled the *Eighth Annual Report of the Bureau of Ethnology to the Secretary of the Smithsonian Institute,* written by J. W. Powell in 1886–87 and printed by the Government Printing Office in 1891. In a chapter on Pueblo architecture, Powell describes kivas in detail. He states that the majority of kivas were totally underground, the hatchways rising approximately eighteen inches above the level of the roof (p. 120). The interiors were plastered smoothly, and, despite this apparent waste of labor, the answer was that kivas had been built of masonry from time immemorial (p. 115). In the West, the woods of cottonwood and pine were used for roof timbers (p.

119). In most cases the depth of the rooms is such that the finished kiva roof does not project above the general level of the ground and is indistinguishable from the adjoining terrain except for the presence of a boxlike projection of masonry that surrounds the entrance trap door and its ladder (p. 113). Explaining the position of the kivas, Powell describes the ideal village plan was to have the house clusters distributed so as to form enclosed courts, with the kivas located within these courts (p. 117). One could conclude from this, according to the number of subterranean rooms reported to have been located under Millboro, that at one time many years ago a well-defined and active Indian village had thrived on the spot.

On one of our trips to Millboro, Smokey Williamson (Samuel) led me to an empty lot next to the fire station. Several persons, including Running Springs, had declared a room to be under this property. When we arrived, we found a concrete, boxlike structure, and when we probed, we hit directly down onto a wooden structure, undoubtedly the roof of the room. When I showed Evie a picture of the concrete, boxlike projection built on the large lot next to the fire station in Millboro, she immediately identified it as being an entrance to a kiva. Admitting it was small, she added that there had been another entrance nearby. Lenette Brychel, as Sally, had said the exact thing earlier—that the entrance under the bed had been small, but the access from the bedroom closet was much larger.

Running Springs declared that there remain about six rooms under the town of Millboro and several more in adjoining areas. According to her, the entire area is a catacomb of tunnels, mostly collapsed today. She further stated that there are some kivas located under the burial mounds in Millboro and that some of the more illustrious chiefs are entombed in them. One time, when she was only about eleven or twelve, Running Springs was raped in a kiva. She became upset and refused to discuss it further and would say only that the offending man was burned to death there in the kiva, and the room was permanently sealed off, never to be used again, as it was impure.

A great Indian master determined where the rooms were to be located. "We built them because the white man was pushing us back, taking our territory. In the early days, we used to scare off the settlers (laughingly). The white man believed in foolish things. Indian warriors would go into the underground rooms and make unearthly, howling noises. I remember the first few white people who came through kept going west, because they thought the area was haunted due to the burial grounds. The braves would let the settlers see them in the woods, then just disappear into the thicket and make weird noises from under the ground. It only worked for a short time but was very effective for awhile!"

In time the Indians allowed the whites to build homes over the rooms, because they knew that the caves were to be used later to help free slaves. "Eventually there were so many whites that we couldn't hide in the rooms anymore, so we gave them to the white man to hide slaves in."

Because there was a good rapport between the Indians and the early settlers, the Indians agreed to build tunnels linking the rooms. "We made them nice, with arched, rounded tops. White man doesn't know how to do that." Running Springs claimed that this "dome" concept made the tunnels much stronger and less likely to collapse.

Her final advice to me was, "Go gentle into the earth; the Great Ones' bones are there. One of the elders died, and we did not want the intruders to ruin his grave like they did our funeral grounds. We made one of the big rooms into a tomb so he will rest undisturbed through all eternity!"

Throughout all these regressions, Running Springs made known her contempt for me: *"Ta-poo-ka"* (talking to me was a necessary evil, a means to an end). Later she said that despite the fact that she found me annoying, *"Kon-tu-ca"* (she had begun to feel more at ease). Her explanation was that she was beginning to realize the workings of my mind.

Running Springs is impatiently waiting for her release. She was left there to guard the kivas and to enlighten, to convince the white man that he can learn to live in harmony with nature. She wants to make certain that the knowledge of the Indian rooms and artifacts gets turned over to the right people, ones who will preserve and revere, not destroy, it! "My only work now is to spread the word of enlightenment. I have talked through others throughout the centuries, but no one listened. About forty years ago, there was a man with long hair, an Indian who lived in southern New York. He got stoned and started talking as Running Springs, no hypnosis involved. Others heard and believed him, but they did not act upon it."

SOARING EAGLE
by Evie Rieder

Who are you?
Where did you come from?
I have known you once before.
I have seen you in my dreams,
eyes wide open.
How is this so?
I have clung to memories
that have no future
and no past.
Now I see you in my present.
Is this real?
Can it last?
Where did you come from?
Did I know you
long ago, on distant thought?
You have touched my soul
somehow.
What is the meaning?
What do you want?

Joann Kelley was born in Murphy, North Carolina,
and is a graduate of the University of Western North Carolina.
Divorced, she is the mother of four children.
She has lived in California since 1964 and is a teacher of
elementary education and a Language Arts Specialist.
As a child she once drove through Virginia
but has never been to Millboro.
In the Millboro story, Joann was Soaring Eagle,
a young brave among the Indians of Robin's Nest,
and a friend of Running Springs.

CHAPTER TWO

THE INDIANS

SOARING EAGLE

DURING A SEMINAR ONE EVENING in San Diego, I was interviewing Running Springs, when suddenly she inquired, "Is there a woman in the room named Anne?" After a short silence, an attractive girl volunteered, "My name is Joann."

When the session ended a short time later, I saw Evie off in one corner of the room speaking earnestly with Joann. Finally she said to me, "Mom, Joann was an Indian back in Robin's Nest with Running Springs. I felt her presence very strongly while I was hypnotized."

Joann Kelley agreed to return to our room with us to be hypnotized. While entranced, she told of seeing many tall trees and an Indian village close by where she lived—only she was a *he* back then—a tall, young brave in his teens! He stated that his name was "Eagle Boy," but later Running Springs explained that his name was really Soaring Eagle, a name too grand for a child; therefore it had evolved to Eagle Boy.

Eagle Boy had heard a lot about white men but seen only a few, as none lived nearby. According to him, the few he had encountered were very friendly.

When asked about Running Springs, he replied, "I know Running Springs. She is very kind, very good, a close friend." The youth was a brave, a hunter, but his burning desire was to study medicine,

19

and Running Springs, though a few years younger than he, was assisting him in this endeavor.

At this point, Evie joined Joann on the bed and was regressed back into the role of Running Springs, then was told, "That is a friend of yours next to you."

Unabashedly she announced, "He loves me!" Then she said something in Indian dialect, and he explained that she had asked him something about his feelings. Running Springs then interjected, "I asked him if he loves me." She continued, *"Tom pooka la poe . . . ici monto!"* (this last said with emphasis). Eagle Boy grinned from ear to ear as Running Springs explained, "I said he is very muscular and handsome." Obviously Eagle Boy understood exactly what she had said.

There were very few white men in the country when Running Springs and Eagle Boy lived, and there was no fighting among the whites that they were aware of. They were from different but closely related tribes, and at that time, they lived down in the valley on the flat land. Their tribes were peaceful, but there existed neighboring tribes who were not friendly and peaceful.

Eagle Boy was killed while still very young, dying in battle with other Indians. Several other young braves were also killed. They had been out on a hunting expedition and were ambushed by another, hostile tribe. Running Springs said sadly, *"Nacho suto,* make a choice to come back to me; *nacho suto,* we will always remain; even in death, we were lovers."

Eagle boy, grinning, answered, *"Ton cooey."* Then he translated: "She enjoyed it." They were both giggling, and I asked if this sort of clandestine romance was legal in their time. Running Springs answered, "No," and Eagle Boy said, "Shussh!" He knew it was wrong and would not be countenanced by either tribe, but he was not going to say anything. The affair went on until he was killed, and after this tragedy Running Springs had no other lovers. Her love for him had been deep and abiding. To Running Springs, Eagle Boy said, *"A whoopa mo who."* Admitting only that it was a term of endearment, they refused to translate it. All Eagle Boy would say was, "It is erotic, an endearment, a manly thing."

In the conscious state, Evie readily admitted, "He was talking about the size of his manhood." They agreed that Running Springs was very outgoing, and that that was what attracted Eagle Boy to her, as he was very shy. He was retiring and hesitant to talk, and Running Springs brought him out of his shell. She, being boisterous and effervescent, had initiated the romance.

Running Springs came from a matriarchal tribe, Eagle Boy from a patriarchal tribe. The thing that most fascinated Soaring Eagle about Running Springs was her assertive independence. None of the women of his tribe dared be like that.

A few weeks after this first encounter, we held another meeting between the two. They were more relaxed the second time, more responsive and at ease with one another.

Running Springs suggested that we simply call him "Eagle," as he would respond to that. She said, "I call him *Koon Cha Ka* (my little Eagle)."

They decided that Springs (as he called her) was about thirteen, and Eagle about sixteen. Their rendezvous were held at the edge of the woods, away from the camp. "When the sun was going down we met. We left in opposite directions and circled back." They were together countless times, and he admitted, "My heart loves her!"

Springs did not worry about becoming pregnant because, as Eagle was quick to point out: "It was before her moons; she was not fully mature." That was why they could not let the tribe know.

Springs said, "I would have been chastised, and Eagle would have been demoted, severely punished." She would have been happy to marry Eagle, but he said, "It would not have been allowed." She was beneath him; they were on different levels. He was a warrior, the chief's son. Besides, they had someone else picked out for him to marry. When asked what her name was, Springs demanded loudly, "Who cares?"

"*Lock Bonga.* Sunflower, that was her name. She wanted him . . ."

"All the women wanted him!" (This last from Springs.)

There were many tribes around there then. (We later decided they had lived during the 1600s.) Eagle explained, "Tribal names were not important. We shared; we lived in harmony." They could intermarry only with permission of the elders, the chiefs.

When the topic of the manhood ritual was introduced, Eagle said he did not consider it very important, but many others did. He had been younger then, about fourteen. The final ceremony was conducted in the kivas, but the more trying test, or "the Quest," was conducted in the mountains. There, alone, he was ordered to prove his hunting ability and was judged by what he brought back.

"Kill something or don't come back," were his orders. After two lonely days in the woods, he brought back a deer he had slain with a bow and arrow. Springs, bursting with pride, interjected, "One shot!" Then she did something that thoroughly amused the onlookers. Pointing one finger, she shot it through the air, simulating an arrow in flight and meanwhile making a "Pssst" sound.

Eagle stated sadly, "I didn't want to kill it . . . those beautiful eyes . . . but I had to." The deer had been full grown, and the boy hunter had an awful job dragging it all the way back to the village.

Eagle's mother had been dead for several years, but his father could scarcely contain his pride in his eldest son. There was a dance, a celebration in the tribal circle, just for the men in the tribe. Several boys were being initiated at that time, but Eagle stood out and was special, not only because he was the chief's son but also because of the size and quality of his quarry. They played drums, rattles, and a flute. Springs explained that this was to call out the spirits. The dance went on all night; it was a big celebration. They ate the deer and drank to the Great Spirit. What did they drink? Springs asked Eagle, "Wasn't it a thick concoction, made from roots, a greyish-green color?" It was a special drink, for the Spirit. When they were asked if the drink was alcoholic, neither of them knew what that meant.

In addition to consuming the thick drink, they smoked a certain weed called Indian tobacco, which had a strange odor. Eagle brought some to share with Springs. "He brought it to me in the woods; we made love all night!" They giggled, and Eagle added, "These were secrets that were never to be shared." The weed was small and fuzzy and resembled dill. They ground it up and put it in a pipe. While high from the weed, they drew pictures on the wall of the room where they met. Discussing this started them giggling again. Eagle said, "They haven't found it yet."

Springs added, "We won't tell you. We left a message in one of the rooms; you will have to find it on your own." By this time they were laughing heartily.

Eagle continued, "You must dig to find the room; if you dig and find the message, it's yours!"

Springs added, "You must find an entrance to the tunnel to get into the room. Shall we give clues? There is a rock in the room from the hillside. We took a stone and scratched a message in the room. There are pictures . . . not lewd."

Springs was giggling by this time, and Eagle adamantly insisted, "I did not!"

Springs countered with, "You did too!" Obviously they had had a very good time together.

Springs declared that Eagle was shy, and Eagle answered, "We did not always agree; my father, my tribe, would not have accepted her. She was what you would call wild, but I had fun with her."

Springs agreed, "Lots of fun! *Mon donga as pee.*"

Eagle answered, "They must not know. *Abunga as pee.*"

Springs translated, "I am telling him I love him still. He understood and answered that they must not find out."

Eagle responded, "*As quaa tha pidda po.* Our hearts are joined forever!"

Springs swore, "*Baa che,* there will be no other, ever (sadly). And when he was killed, there was no other, ever." She was absolutely devastated when he died.

Eagle was asked why Springs had been instructed to remain in the area of Robin's Nest, and he explained, "It was her responsibility to remain there; her energy remains there. If she really wanted to leave, she could, but she knows that her quest is not finished, not complete. After the white woman goes back to Virginia (the author) and exposes the remains of our culture, then Springs will leave. Yes, once we have completed this mission, our culture will be known to others. There is a purpose, there is a reason."

After that mission is complete, Running Springs will still be available for consultation, but according to Eagle there will no longer be a reason to contact her. A part of her energy remains there, and when that energy is released, she can leave. Springs continued to explain, "She wants the people to go in and preserve the kivas, expose them to people who study, the many tunnels and rooms. Her spirit is in one of the kivas. They burned her body, put her ashes in a kiva."

Eagle said, "I see a concrete box."

Springs answered, *"La puent ta qua."*

Eagle reminded her that it was the wrong dialect. She spoke four; he spoke only three. Springs stated that sometimes they had trouble communicating, so between the two of them, they formed their own language.

In camp they ignored each other. Her duties were grinding corn, watching the children, hauling the water, making the food.

I asked Eagle what he did when not hunting, other than standing around and looking pretty. Springs turned on me in a fury and hissed, "Don't you make fun of him!"

Eagle answered that he worked with his father, who was teaching him healing, and that Springs was teaching him, too. They figured that if both of them eventually became healers, then perhaps they could be together. Springs thought that maybe his fiancée, Sunflower, would perhaps just go away.

"Some Indian groups will fight us (about) exposing the kivas," Eagle explained. "The spirit always lives. There will be a few who do not understand, but it shall be accomplished. Eventually there will be a big archaeology dig there; it will be a psychic dig."

When he finished this spiel, Springs, shrugging her shoulders, turned to me and observed, adoration dripping from her voice, "Isn't he great?"

As an afterthought, he added, "Running Springs will lead the dig. She was chosen because she has no fear; she is not afraid."

Running Springs explained that she was deeply in love with Eagle, and "When you free me, I will go to him."

Eagle confirmed this, saying, "We are one. Yes, I will be waiting; she knows where to go. We are all one, total oneness with the universe." Turning to Springs, he said with great feeling: "May light speed you!"

WHITE STAR

One afternoon I received a call from a girl in Elsinore named Kathi Shannon. She had just finished reading *Mission to Millboro* and was thoroughly intrigued by the story. She felt she might be involved in it. Hypnosis proved her to be correct.

Her name was White Star, and she could see herself at about age sixteen in a long leather skirt, walking along a path. She was hauling water, a pole resting across her shoulders with a skin-type bucket at either end. The Indian village was atop a high hill or mountain, and there was a solid forest of trees on all sides—maple, birch, oak, pines. She could see tepees and one wickiup, made from hides. Looking down into the valley below, she could clearly see the town of Millboro. There were probably a hundred or more Indians living in the village. The living area was back off the main road, and there were three separate, cleared areas. The camp was multitribal, and even though the remnants of several tribes grouped together for protection, they still sought to retain their individual tribal identities. There was a large, cleared, round area used for powwows and other ceremonies. (This large round area was later located by the author on a trip to Millboro.) Singing Bird and White Eagle had been married there. When the name of Singing Bird was introduced to White Star, she asked, "Wasn't she part white?" They had all looked forward very much to the wedding; it was one of the biggest events ever to take place in Robin's Nest, and months of planning and preparation went into it.

White Star came to Robin's Nest with her family when she was very young. "We had to come there from somewhere else to hide from the white men. We came there because it was far away from the authorities. We came from the North; people traveled South because the North was getting too populated. Came to avoid being put onto a reservation."

When she was still very young, her mother died, and she and her older brother were raised by their father, not unlike Kathi's life today. "She was one of the children whom the storytellers would take care of while the father was off hunting or working in the fields." This last remark was from Running Springs who, at this

Kathie Shannon was born in Redwood City,
California. She attended school in Sunnyvale,
California, and Kodiak, Alaska.
Married, with one child,
Kathie has worked as a barber and is
currently training to be a hypnotherapist.
She has lived in California for ten years and
has never been to Virginia.
In the story she is White Star, who lived in
the Indian village at Robin's Nest, above Millboro.

point, was regressed with White Star. Even though Running Springs lived many years before White Star, she was able to see all that transpired, from her lifetime until the time the Indians were made to leave Robin's Nest, a couple of hundred years later. She continued, "She had a brother who was a few years older, and he would get so *pissed* at her. She would get her moccasins on the wrong feet or break her beads, and he was always on her case, demanding, Why do you *do* that? She would just look at him and smile, and he would relent and say, That's all right, and proceed to pick up whatever was broken. She was very cute."

One of the things White Star enjoyed doing was smashing the corn. Most others hated the job, but she took a perverse pleasure in it. The corn was then baked into a hard, tasteless bread that all agreed was awful.

She discussed the large, white rock that Singing Bird first mentioned in *Mission to Millboro* and many have discussed since. "It is cleared around the rock; it stands on the edge of a ledge on one side and has a little bit of a slope connected to it, so you can stand in front of it. We used to try to climb it. It is like a landmark; people meet there, etc. Rocks and trees have a lot of significance to us, and that's a very special rock. There is some sort of legend about that rock."

When she was in her late teens, she married Dancing Bear, who was a hunter. It was an extremely happy marriage that produced three children.

By the time White Star matured, there were no tribes left anywhere in the area, as the Indians had all been forced out of their homes. All that were left were the few clusters of "runners," like the group that inhabited Robin's Nest for so many happy years.

White Star died shortly before the Indians were forced out of Robin's Nest. She said there was a lot of talk before she died about them having to leave, and most of the elders were very worried. She had a happy life, and her one regret was that she died at age twenty-seven, much too young, orphaning her three children.

The room in which she died was a cavelike room, up on a hill above the camp. It had been dug into the side of a hill, with grass above. It had a dirt floor, dirt walls, a wooden roof, and carpet on the floor—very small, about the size of a one car garage. Because it had a large side opening, it could not be classified as a kiva. With her, attending her, was an older woman who was very sad. "There is something in my chest; something is pressing down on my chest."

It had been a happy though brief life, and White Star was glad she had escaped the wrenching, traumatic move when the surviving Indians were forcibly marched out of the mountain paradise onto a hot, dusty, dry, miserable reservation.

SNOWBIRD

After two sessions with Joann Kelley, she told me that she had met a girl at the seminar in San Diego whom she felt strongly was also in this story. Contacting the girl was relatively simple, as she lives in nearby Temecula.

Cassie is her name, and, for personal reasons, she decided not to be identified in the story. Because there is illness in her family, she was able to come for only one hypnosis session—but that one session proved very interesting.

The girl regressed back into the life of an Indian squaw named Snowbird.

We first talked to her when she was about six or seven. Snowbird was feisty, a tomboy who played strenuous games with her boy cousins. Orphaned, she lived with an aunt and uncle in a building made of hides, not a tepee, more like an A-frame, with furs on the floor to sleep on. Between her aunt and uncle and the three boy cousins and herself, she exclaimed, "It is crowded in there!"

Living in the Indian village high on the hill, she was well aware of the village of Millboro below, but "I stay away from there. I was told to stay away. My cousins sneak down and look at those people; sometimes I go along—it's fun to look. They are different, those people. They don't come up here."

Snowbird helped take care of the younger children, but her primary work was with her aunt, who was a healer. She loved the healing work. They raised herbs for medicine and stripped bark off the trees. The healing work fascinated her, but at heart she was still very young, and besides, she wanted to horse around with her cousins. When she was horsing around, she could not stay focused, which resulted in her being chastised and shaken. Sometimes it was hard to learn the names of all the plants, and she would become confused.

Little (or White) Eagle lived in the village at that time, and Snowbird said he was training to be a shaman. He became very upset when his wife, Singing Bird, was made to leave the tribe and move into the village.

Snowbird was aware of the underground rooms. "I smell a really dank smell, an earthen smell. It frightens me. We kept some herbs down there, and sometimes I have to go down there and get them." She was aware of one large room with another, smaller room nearby. It was the smaller one that was used for herbal storage. "They weren't touched by regular people; just special people could touch them. We cared for them, made sure they were dry and that no animals came near them."

Occasionally she was ordered to go to the sulfur pool and get some water for use in the medicine. "It was warm—I didn't like to go there, didn't like the water on me, the way it felt or smelled. Some of the older people get into the warm water; they like it. I hope I will never have to do that."

The young, intrepid Indian girl went all over the mountaintop and to some places she was not supposed to go, but fortunately she was never caught.

The farming and growing of crops was handled by other women in the tribe; Snowbird never had any part of that. She declared, "It seems like we grew a tough corn. It was different; you had to grind it with stones. I had to do that sometimes. Grinding herbs was fun; grinding that corn was not."

Her life on the hill had been extremely happy but short. She died suddenly at about age sixteen of a fever, before the Indians were made to leave their mountaintop paradise. "I remember the older people being worried, and people talking about having to leave. I sensed sadness. Things got serious; people came and went, their faces solemn. There was a sadness, an air of apprehension over the tribe. White men came then. They did not camp in our place; about one-half the way up the mountain they camped, to watch us."

In her opinion, the white men wore ugly clothing, ugly, and it smelled bad—a brown leather vest thing with no arms, long pants, boots, and something funny on their heads—and they carried guns.

It had been a good, happy life for Snowbird, and she died just before it became ugly. She was not especially impressed with the beauty of Robin's Nest, because she thought the whole world was like that—she had never seen any place else.

In the conscious state, Cassie volunteered that the bread made from that corn tasted awful!

ROY
by Evie Rieder

If ever once
there was a way
I could say
what I want to say,
I think the time
would have to be today.

And if at
such a time
I can't
find my mind,

Don't turn me off,
in time
I'll be fine.

Sometimes I stumble
ahead in my brain.
Words come out wrong
and the feelings change.
Jumbled emotions
and strained
points of view.
I realize they can't
mean much to you.

But you've got
to look deeper
inside my eyes,
you'll see that's where
my sincerity lies.

Lynn Farmer was born in Los Angeles
and was raised in Gardena, California.
Her profession is Engineering Services Administrator.
She had never been to Virginia prior to this research.
Her role in the story is Martha.

CHAPTER THREE

ROY AND MARTHA

WHEN I HYPNOTIZED Evie for therapeutic reasons and instructed her to regress into a happy, fulfilled life, she immediately started talking about Roy Farmer, who lived in the Williamsville area and who died just prior to the Civil War. Evie was the first person in this group to regress into the life of a member of the opposite sex.

Roy Farmer was a glib, outspoken, salty character, whose raison d'etre was his wife, Martha. He adored her. Soon he revealed that Martha today was Lynn Farmer, Evie's current roommate. The two were hypnotized first individually, then jointly, and the following is the story they told.

They met in a fairly large city in Virginia, possibly Richmond. Martha's family had recently moved to Virginia from Pittsburgh, Pennsylvania. Besides her parents, there were three girls and two boys in the family, Martha being the middle sister. Roy was a recent immigrant of Welsh descent, who had come alone from Ireland to America at age twenty-two. He was totally uneducated. He spotted Martha riding through town with her two sisters in a buggy. "She had on this lovely blue bonnet. She shone like the sun, like a diamond."

Martha was aware of him, but she was careful not to let him know that she had noticed him. "Roy wasn't a real good-looking man, but he had his points, and once you got to know him, you found him attractive."

Their original meeting was in the general store, and each week, probably on Saturday afternoon, Roy would go into town hoping to find her. He went into the saloon to wait, but he refrained from drinking because Martha was very proper. "I would sit in the bar and wait for her, then I would casually go over there, to the store. She was the middle sister, and they wouldn't give me no room." Martha, giggling, stated that her sisters were very protective.

The sisters took up their posts, one on either side of Martha to keep Roy at bay, but eventually he managed to talk to Martha and ingratiate himself with her. "They didn't think I was good enough for her, and I probably wasn't."

Roy already had his spread, his homestead, in the Green Valley area, and the house was nearly finished, but "I stayed there until I got what I wanted. We knew each other about six months before we got married. She ran off with me against the wishes of her parents and her sisters. Her dad knew that I was an honorable man."

Martha added, "They knew that he would take care of me, but he was just so rough around the edges that the others just couldn't see what I could."

Roy stated, "Martha polished me."

They were married in a church nearby, probably the old Williamsville church, in the year 1819, around the 5th of September. In addition to the minister and a couple of black people, some of Roy's local friends attended. Martha's family refused to come for the event, but she thought one of her sisters had arrived at the last minute. "They just didn't understand the South; they thought it was really backward." Her name she thought had been Heath, or possibly Harris, which is Lynn's mother's maiden name today.

It was about a year before the first son, Matthew, was born. Over the course of about fifteen years, three more children arrived—Adam, Samuel, and baby Eve. Roy stated proudly, "Martha knew how to make babies wait," and Martha explained, "I understood the woman's cycle, and when she was more likely to conceive." Roy concluded, pride spilling out of him, that Martha was a good woman who was very well educated and that she taught him a lot.

The couples farm consisted of "ten plots." Evie later conjectured that Roy had probably owned around 100 acres. There were trees all around it. "I didn't even have to put up a fence; the trees keep the cows and the herds in. I got over 200 head of cattle. There's a pond on my land which is drying up. Up front there's a fenced area where we keep the horses and pigs."

Until just prior to his death at age sixty-two, Roy was a very happy, contented man. We talked to him at about age forty-two, and his life was placid. The main concern he expressed was the oldest boy, Matthew. "He's out of control, over twenty-one, and I can't do nothin' with him. He's a liberal, wants to be a lawyer, is against this Confederacy thing. Went up North to get rid of his southern accent. It does not please me, but it pleases Martha."

He loved Martha dearly. "She cooks the best dumplins ever made, and bread, sourdough. That's new; they just brought that over from France. She makes me feel so good, rubs my feet at night." Their romantic life was great. "In the beginning it was better, but Martha gets kinda tired. I understand she's a woman, and she gets them mood swings. Just being next to her gives me all the satisfaction I need."

Awhile back a horse had stepped on his foot, causing permanent damage and incessant pain. However, "the doc gave me these pills to take or just liquid I drink. It's got more than a little alcohol in it and I think some of that . . . morphine. Martha don't like me to take it because I'm no good when I do. Most of the time I'm able to drive the horse with the plow." Changing the subject abruptly, he continued, talking about his favorite subject. His face lit up whenever he talked about his daughter. "Eve is growing up; she's about seven now . . . she's the prettiest little thing. Martha makes her clothes. None of our kids went to school; Martha teaches them at home (proudly). Martha knows how to read and write and do her numbers. She can do just about anything."

The next time I talked to Roy, he was about fifty-two. Baby Eve was about thirteen and still his darlin'. Matthew was a lawyer up in the North, in one of those uppity towns, probably in New York state. A real high-paid lawyer, Matthew was, and he sent money home quite often. Samuel and Adam were tending the farm, as Roy's foot was still bad, and he did not do much anymore. Smugly, he agreed that he was a pretty successful farmer, pretty comfortable. Samuel and Adam were eighteen and sixteen respectively, and Samuel was seeing a woman in town, an older woman in her late twenties or early thirties. Martha did not know this, and they were not going to tell her, as she would not like it.

They had an active social life, had neighbors over, went to others' homes. There were dances and barn raisings, and once a month there was a regular party somewhere. Martha was inclined to be bored by most of the womenfolk, as they lacked her education. "They were little, domesticated things, and nice, but so boring. There is so much more to life than just home and children, but they just don't seem to understand that."

Both loved to dance, and despite his injured foot, Roy managed to dance a lot in his own, inimitable way. He explained, "Sometimes it was a big circle and sometimes just separate. No square dancing. We did a lot of this (thrashing her arms up and down) and twirling around. Music was usually a banjo, a picking thing, a straight thing, harmonica, and definitely a fiddle."

He did not hit the booze: Martha did not like him to drink. Martha intervened, "People got so *stupid* when they drank; it was disgusting!" Roy had done a lot of drinking prior to meeting Martha, and she explained it was because he had been so lonely.

They knew the older, white-haired man, who lived in the Green Valley plantation house, and his wife. Roy made a disgusted face and, when asked why he did not like the man, readily replied: "Well, he runs the whole damn county! He's got slaves all over the place, and I don't believe in slaves. I use the Indians. They help me, and Martha gives them eggs and milk. I don't believe (whispering, very confidentially) . . . you can't tell nobody this . . . I don't believe in men as cattle. You don't *own* men!" When I mentioned that the old man in the plantation house was very active in the Underground Railroad, Roy dismissed it immediately with, "I don't want to talk about that!" In a quieter tone, he added, "Ask Martha."

As we heard from the people in Millboro, the Green Valley Farm was in those days the site of many successful social functions.

Martha recalled going there several times, "The parties would start outside in the daytime, with a lot of cooking and eating, and then we would move inside for dancing later. The old, white-haired man and others in the house were very nice, extremely generous." When it was mentioned to her that Roy did not seem to care much for the man, she replied, "I don't think there's too many people he does like, really. He's suspicious." The party Martha described sounded very much like the Guy Fawkes celebration (discussed in detail in *Mission to Millboro),* but Martha denied any knowledge of Fawkes. That party must have been strictly endemic to Millboro.

The highlight of their life was the occasional trip into town, which was several miles away (probably either Millboro or Warm Springs). Martha explained, "When we go into town, we take all day to do it. Not that the trip is so long, it's just that we do it so seldom, we make a whole day out of it."

As was the case in most communities in those days, serious social life revolved around the church. According to Roy, the old Williamsville church had been bi-denominational, Baptist and Presbyterian. They took turns using the building.

The old church, the one in which Roy and Martha were married, was white with a green tower. It looked like the Presbyterian Church today, near where Grandma's house had stood in Millboro. Martha sees "a white church with steps going up the front—a white, wooden building, long and narrow." Roy said that winds took the old church; it was blown over, and that is why they built the new one of brick, and lower, so that when the strong winds come down the valley, that could not recur.

Roy was not an ardent churchgoer. In fact, this was probably the only thing Roy and Martha ever had any serious fights about. "She says, Oh, Roy, why don't you come with me? She reads from the Bible every night before we go to bed. It don't hurt me any, that's what she says, but I don't rightly buy it." His excuse was that the farm needed him; there was just too much work waiting for him to waste time at church. Occasionally, one or both of the boys would beg off from church, using the same reason, when they could get away with it. He kept peace at home by going with Martha about every six weeks or so. The congregation was primarily women and children, numbering between twenty and thirty. Roy disliked the minister. "He's too liberal for my blood. He's going to get into trouble; he likes the niggers." When Roy was asked if he was a Confederate sympathizer, he became very angry and answered loudly, *"I am not a Confederate!* I just don't believe in sticking your nose where it don't belong. I've made my peace with the world, and I'm happy, and that's all I want. I've been pushed around all my life, and I've made my peace with the world, don't want no trouble. I see what's comin'!"

The two decided that Sunday was their best day. According to Roy, "Martha would take the children to church; I would take a bath. She'd come home, and we would do our duty." There was lots of giggling at the obvious reference to their sex life. Occasionally, they bickered. Roy stated, "She used to hit me with a wooden spoon!"

Laughing followed this statement, and Martha explained, "Roy only bathed once a week. He'd get all stinky out there working, and then he'd come in trying to get close to me, and I'd tell him to go take a bath!"

Then Roy reiterated, "She'd slap be with that wooden spoon, on the hands."

CHAPTER FOUR

THE CHURCH

ROY'S ATTITUDE REGARDING the Underground Railroad activity taking place in the area was, "I don't want to talk about it! I just don't want no trouble." One of his first statements to me was, "I saw it coming, knew those niggers were goin' to cause trouble. A lot of things led up to it; the South, we could feel it comin' for a long time. Martha told me there was goin' to be a struggle the minute this president got in. Not Lincoln, the one before him [Buchanan]. He was a wishy-washy ass; he wouldn't make any definite plans. We saw the blockades comin'; there was just too much happening." According to Roy and Martha, Buchanan definitely did not know what he was doing. Roy said, "His attitude was that the land belonged to the white man, and anyone, black or red, who got in the way, would be destroyed. He kowtowed to the South, and this was because the rich planation owners bought him off." They both felt he was largely responsible for the Civil War, and Roy ended the discussion with, "He drank a lot, too."

From studying reports of the Buchanan administration, Roy and Martha's statements appear to be true. Some historians offer the opinion that it was Buchanan's soft stand on slavery that led to the war.

Both were in absolute accord that there was at least one large, secret room under the church in Williamsville, where slaves and Union soldiers were hidden. The room is located in the right rear as one faces the church, and was entered through a tunnel leading from the hill behind the church down into the room. The mouth of the tunnel was hidden by moss and a large tree with drooping branches. According to Roy, the Indians did not build the room; the work was done primarily by Negroes. There was a road that crossed the hill above the church, and "you could drive a horse and wagon or buggy right up over it, and anybody getting out of the wagon wouldn't be seen; they'd just jump right into the cavity and disappear."

The original church had been built up off the ground, and to get into the room one went down some stairs until they veered to the left. There, to the right, was a part brick, part wooden wall. Roy explained, "There's a certain brick; you pull that brick out. That's the lock. The wall slides to the left; it's a big door; it's wide. The church used to store all kinds of stuff down there. This has always been a Yankee church—they stored bedding and extra rifles in that room. The room is part under the church, and part of it is off, back and behind."

Underground Railroad activity had not always frightened Roy. He had taken part in building the room that was installed under the old church, "I put in the pulleys from the tracks, so you could pull the wall back that allowed you to get down into the room." In 1850, when the Fugitive Slave Act passed and the penalty for assisting slaves to escape was thousands of dollars plus long jail sentences, Roy's attitude modified significantly. He stated, "We could lose everything . . . everything. It's just not worth it!"

Martha, however, remained steadfast in her determination to free slaves or Union soldiers or whoever else needed freeing. "I want to say it's like a fight between my heart and my head, like I want to help them and should; it's the Lord's work." She took eggs and milk everywhere she went, especially during the war years. To help feed the poor souls huddled under the church, she also contributed bacon, dried meat, and with Roy's concurrence, money. "We had too much food, and giving it away was God's work. We went without a great abundance because we gave it to others, but we always had more than plenty."

The newer brick church that stands today is built directly on the ground, negating the need for stairs. Martha claimed that there was a trap door in the right rear corner of the church, behind the pews. "The women would have sewing fests during the week. We were always up in that right corner, near the trap door. We kept it open only long enough to take food and medical care down to the people below. We would drape our quilts and other sewing in such a way that if someone came into the church and the door was open, they couldn't see the door, and we would have time to cover it."

The trap door was about two-and-a-half by three feet and lifted up towards the rear of the church. Similar to the trap door in Grandma's house in Millboro, a small, rectangular piece of wood, about six inches by nine inches, was pried out of the floor, exposing a handle that was used to raise the door. Nothing about the door was visible to the naked eye, and the plug of wood was covered with a movable pew or, more likely, a piano bench, when the door was closed.

Several steps led down into the room below. Martha said, "There's a pipe in the yard outside that supplied air into the room. I remember thinking that if it rained, water would go down that pipe. It got very stuffy down there at times, despite the air pipe. No animals came down; the tunnel was not that open. It was covered with natural shrubs and tree roots. We got little rabbits, small stuff, that was no bother." (Author's note: On a recent trip to Williamsville, we found the pipe that Martha mentioned. However, on our next trip, we discovered it was gone.)

Sometimes, in the manner of the church in Millboro, they would bring the refugees out of hiding on Sunday morning, right after services, while there was a lot of commotion. Other times, if there was a large potluck dinner or some such affair being held in the churchyard, they would spirit refugees to awaiting wagons. According to Martha, "Most people at the functions did not know who these people were. We told them they were people who were less fortunate than we were, and, because we were a church, we should be open and giving to them. They were dressed raggedy, and the local people would feel sorry for them. They would walk in groups, and folks at the church would think they knew them. Someone would say, "Oh yes, I know him; he's so and so who lives in such a place." It would throw the others off.

They stopped all underground activity in the church when it was occupied during the war. Martha thought they had probably sealed off the entrance at the mouth of the tunnel. The arrogance of the soldiers on both sides upset Martha greatly and kept her angry a good deal of the time. The injustices they committed made her "want to jump up and accost the buggers, but of course I couldn't do that." At one instance, some soldiers rode their horses right into the church, an act from which the outraged parishioners never recovered. This incident is described in Richard Armstrong's book, *Ambush at Williamsville, Virginia* (Minuteman Press, Staunton, VA, 1986).

When little Eve was about nineteen, she died from consumption [tuberculosis], and Roy died two years later from a broken heart. Martha explained, "He was just crazy about her; she was so beautiful and was developing into such a beautiful woman. He was so proud of her. She was the fruit of his loins, and for her to be so ill, it just killed him. He still had me and the boys—he had a lot—there was no reason for him to do that. He just drowned in his grief!"

Martha lived on past the age of eighty. The oldest boy returned home for the funerals of his sister and father. "He came back and hugged me, and I was glad he was there, but he was not the same boy who left. He dressed real fancy, had his own world. Both Roy and I suspected he spied for the North during the war, but we never really *knew* that."

The two remaining sons stayed with their mother and ran the farm. When they married, their families remained on the homestead. Martha said she saw many grandchildren running about. Despite her sons and their families, she was consumed with loneliness, "I kept busy, but once in a while I would think, why did it have to be this way? I was so contented at one time, so happy. Roy was such a good man."

Roy and Martha had a true, abiding love. According to Martha, "A lot of people at that time got married when they found someone they weren't totally repulsed by. Love was not the question, if you could just find someone you could get along with. Very few found real, true love. Our attraction was so strong; that's what made our life so good." She lamented about the people who lived during that sad time, "The tragedy they witnessed—no one should have to live through what the Negroes and the people caught up in that war did!"

In the conscious state, Lynn explained that the church women had quilting bees and similar activities to cover up their Underground involvement. They did not do any cooking at the church, but all the women had large families, and cooking in huge quantities went on all the time. Having extra food was no problem. They would bring the food from home and smuggle it into the church in baskets and hampers that ostensibly carried sewing things. The women were all the same—strong, dedicated farm women who knew that everything that was currently going on politically was against God's will and that they were doing the Lord's work in fighting it.

Lenette Brychel was born in Chicago, Illinois. Her profession is that of Property Auditor Inspector. She is also a professional psychic. Lenette currently lives in Las Vegas, Nevada, and has visited Lake Elsinore twice. She has never been to Virginia and her role in the story is that of Sally, young granddaughter of "Grandma" (Bertha "Bertie" Cullins or Collins), who used to help her grandmother hide Negroes and Union soldiers in the hidden rooms under Grandma's house.

Author standing on porch of the old boarding house in Millboro. Director Sean McNamara and Sightings *crew below.*

Photo by Margo Oxendine.

Picture of hidden room under the property where "Grandma's" house stood, taken from a hole the owner made in the side of the room. Note the mouth of the tunnel and the collapsed support beam. The tube sticking out of the debris has been identified as a "speaking tube."

Picture of the hidden room taken from a small hole in the top of the room. One can clearly see the wooden, beamed ceiling.

Hole found by the owner of the property where "Grandma's" house was located, when he tore down the old shed.

Ditch that the property owner dug with his backhoe, so that the author could take pictures of the hidden room.

Site where Grandma's house stood.
Hidden room, or kiva, is located directly in front of the shed
at the rear of the property.

CHAPTER FIVE

SALLY

Lenette Brychel has been a friend of Joe Nazarowski's for many years. She knew him when they both lived in Chicago, Illinois. When she saw a TV show about the Millboro story, she felt that somehow she was a part of it. Currently she lives in Las Vegas, Nevada, and one weekend when she was visiting her sister in California, she drove to Lake Elsinore and contacted Joe. He brought her in to be hypnotized.

Claiming to be about eight years old, she said her name was Sally and that she lived with her Grandma in a small town in Virginia, surrounded by mountains and with a railroad coming into town. Her whole life had been in that town, because her parents had died when she was a baby and Grandma was raising her.

When asked what she was doing, we heard, "Can't get past where I am standing, right in front of the general store. I see three steps, and I want to go up into the store. It's a grocery store, and I want to go into it, because there's candy in that store!"

Looking around the town, she said that she could see the corral with the "horse man" in it, working with the horses. She identified the man as Joe today. She further explained that the young girl had a powerful crush on Charley, or the "horse man," and used to spend a lot of time at the edge of the corral, watching him work.

Then she volunteered, "There was a lady I was afraid of. She was small, had long dark hair, and acted strange. She was mean and liked to pull my hair." Undoubtedly, the woman she was describing was Ava, Constance's mother, who was definitely one of the stranger women in the town.

Sally attended school and knew Phebe Ailstock, Becky's oldest daughter.

Grandma was very deeply involved in smuggling Negroes through that town, and Sally used to help her.

"The floor would come up; there was a hidden room under the house. Grandma would take down blankets and food, and everybody knew they were safe there. They came in the back way, where nobody could see them. There was like . . . a doorway . . . and it led down into the room. (Author's note: Sally was aware of both of the tunnels, but it is clear that she had no knowledge of where the longer one came in from.) The house is right in town. If you go in back of the store, it's up on a hill." She saw the house as still being there today.

"I can see white, like a frame house. It was not real white then. It was like it needed to be painted. It is whiter now. The room is still there. People who have lived there were unaware of the room or what it was used for."

She used to go down into the hidden room and play with the kids.

"I liked the black kids, the black people; they were fun. During the war there were mostly Union soldiers down there. There is a fireplace in the dining room; that's where the trap door is. The door was about two-and-a-half to three feet square, and the stairs were very steep. They were made of wood and were permanent steps, very old and decrepit. There was no handrail—I used to scoot down the steps one at a time on my butt. Sometimes they took the people out in wagons, sometimes on horseback."

Sally had trouble seeing the shed at the rear of the property, but at a later time Honey (Millie Sproule) described it as small and made of wood, falling apart now. Evidently Sally was not allowed into that shed, but Honey had been there and said, "There was a trap door in the floor of the shed. You had to move sacks of grain, then lift up the trap door. The tunnel has caved in, some of it. A lot of dirt has gotten into the tunnel."

Sally continued, "There was another little room off of the main room, like a small basement. There was some kind of light, a lantern, perhaps. It was cold and damp, and I see a lot of torn sheets to bind up wounds. When anyone died, they were taken into that room. Probably where the slop buckets, or chamber pots, were, too."

Sally said, "To open the trap door, you had to move the table, roll up the rug, and even if you did this you could not see the trap door; it just blended in with the wooden floor."

Sally was a very sickly child. This she admitted, and it was reaffirmed by Honey, who had been a good friend of Grandma's. Honey took any and all food that was left over from the restaurant every night to Grandma, to help feed the people down below. Sally died at age thirteen from smallpox. Grandma was hiding her at home when it happened. Because smallpox is so contagious, Sally was supposed to go to the hospital or be quarantined somewhere, but Grandma would not do that, feeling she could take better care of Sally at home. Because of the way she died, the young girl was cremated.

Later, in the conscious state, Lenette marked an X on a large, white house in the picture of old Millboro, saying it had been her Grandma's house.

In June of 1992, the author went to Millboro with director Sean McNamara of the *Sightings* show of Fox Television.

Prior to that trip, I had heard from a realtor in Hot Springs, Virginia, that the old house identified by Lenette had burned down a couple of years ago. A few days later he called me to say that the new owner of the property had gone in with his backhoe and torn out the foundation.

Shortly thereafter, the new owner called to say that in tearing out the old shed, he had found a hole in the ground and that it appeared that there was either a room or tunnel below.

Before leaving for Virginia, I telephoned Lenette and hypnotized her right over the phone. The following is what I heard.

"In the dining room, there is a fireplace. It used to be used, but it has been sealed off, no longer functional. About three feet in front of the fireplace is the trap door. In the floor is a small, crescent-shaped piece of wood about six or eight inches long; it looks like part of the floor. You have to take a sharp object to pry it up; we used to use a kitchen knife. Then you reach into the hole, and to the right there's a rope, a thick, heavy rope. You pull the rope, and the trap door comes up. The room under the dining room is the larger room. There's a second, smaller room under the yard, to the rear between the house and the shed. It has a dirt floor, bilious green rock or concrete walls. Looks like a mine; ceiling is shored up with boards across the top. There's a rope; don't know what it's there for. There is more than one tunnel; the tunnels are reinforced with wood. There's a lantern, an oil lamp hanging from the rope." She mentioned that she could see the shed clearly, that this was the first time she had seen the shed when hypnotized.

In Virginia, Larry Fresh, a local realtor, affirmed that there had been a fireplace in the dining room and that the fireplace had been sealed up for years. This he knew because he had sold the place several times. He also recalled being aware of a dip or bowing in the floor directly in front of the fireplace.

For some reason, the hole under the shed had been made smaller, too small for a man to pass through. Probably this was done when it was used as a privy. Therefore, the present property owner dug a ditch a few feet alongside the room and pounded a very small hole, about the size of a pie pan, through the wall.

It is hard to describe the surprise and shock everyone present felt when I crawled into that ditch and shone a very powerful light into the small hole. There I saw a room, much larger than I had imagined. The first thing to greet my eyes was a bilious green, concrete wall; then, raising the light, I saw a heavy, thick, wood-beamed ceiling. The wood is glossy and shiny, and I thought perhaps it had become petrified. Later I was told by Running Springs that the resin-like compound the Indians painted on the wood made it shiny.

The floor was dirt, and a few tree roots had made their way into the room. A few feet away from the large compost heap (put there when the privy was in operation) was a large pile of empty bottles.

Those bottles may be a souvenir of prohibition days, or, as some of the townfolk have reasoned, they may have been left there by hiding Confederate deserters, who did a lot of drinking to pass away long days and even longer nights.

There have been innumerable times during this research when active chills have played up and down my spine. This was most certainly one of those times! Because of poor lighting, it was difficult to get good photos, but one that I took very clearly displays the mouth of a collapsed tunnel.

The question has been asked as to why anyone would go to the expense and backbreaking work to install such a room as this, way back before the time of bulldozers and power tools. One bystander asked, "Why would people back before the Civil War go to such work and expense to build these rooms just to help escaping slaves?" I asked this person how long he thought that slavery had existed prior to the Civil War. His answer was, "Oh, I dunno, about ten or fifteen years?"

What must be considered is that no one ever foresaw the end of slavery, least of all the slaves themselves. Many generations of blacks were born into slavery, worked as slaves all their lives, and died in slavery. Slavery in some form existed in this country from its inception until 1863. Even Abraham Lincoln had no thought of freeing slaves when he became president. He clearly stated that he had no intention of interfering with slavery in the existing slave states, but he vowed to fight its spread into incoming states. A great many sincere, dedicated Christians devoted their entire lives to the freeing of those slaves. An exemplification of that devotion is the network of rooms and tunnels built under the town of Millboro.

*Israel A.M.E. Church
in Albany, New York*

*Historic site plaque on the church grounds of
the Israel A.M.E. Church, Albany, New York*

Israel A.M.E. Church in Albany, New York. This panel under the staircase may be a sealed-up entrance to a hidden room. The bricked-up area at the right was probably an old coal bin.

*Rear door of the Israel A.M.E. Church.
The angled wall forms an entryway well-hidden from the street.*

CHAPTER SIX

SLAVERY

THE REACTION OF THE AVERAGE, Northern white to slavery, prior to the passage of the Fugitive Slave Act in 1850, was one of apathy. For the most part, they were opposed to the institution of slavery in principle, but not vehemently so. As long as it was kept in the South and out of sight, it was out of mind.

The Underground Railroad (UGRR) existed to some extent in every state north of the border slave states. According to some authors, the largest number of slaves escaped into Ohio, because the Ohio River, running for more than 200 miles, borders both Kentucky and Virginia. The college at Oberlin, Ohio, one of the first in the country to admit black students, was dedicated to abolition, and it has been said that the entire town was a station on the UGRR. The town of Oberlin lies almost due north of Millboro, Virginia. It is estimated that more than 100,000 blacks escaped slavery with the help of the UGRR.

Books and articles concerning the underground movement, to a large extent, have been authored by blacks. The safest havens for escaping slaves were the black communities in Northern states, comprised primarily of former slaves. Some had bought their freedom, some were given freedom by their owners, and some had escaped bondage so long ago that their owners had long since given up retrieving them. All escaping slaves faithfully followed the North star, and a slave's education, such as it was, was not complete until he could locate the North star and keep it in his sight.

Most colorful and outstanding among Negroes who fought slavery was an inauspicious, plain-looking woman named Harriet Tubman. Dubbed "Moses" by her people, Tubman, after her original escape, made nineteen forays back into the South and led over 300 of her people to freedom.

Born about 1821 on the eastern shore of Maryland, Tubman, faced with the threat of being sold by her master in about 1845, left and made her way, alone, to Philadelphia and freedom.

When returning South, she was always armed with two items, opium with which to drug babies and small children until they were out of danger, and a small pistol to threaten any slave who changed his mind and decided to return to his master. She threatened to kill them before she would allow them to return, because a defecting slave was a threat to the entire underground operation.

Her greeting when approaching an underground terminal was, "I am a friend with friends."

A signal widely used to reassure others was a right hand to the ear, grasping the rim of the ear between the thumb and forefinger. A hand held up with palm extended outward was a sign of imminent danger. The average distance between UGRR stations was approximately twelve miles, and occasionally wagon owners temporarily shod the feet of their horses with carpeting to eliminate noise in the dead of night.

There was at least $40,000 in rewards offered for Harriet Tubman by unhappy Southern planters. She is said to have been a master of disguise and, along with others in the underground, employed the use of wigs, costumes, and veils, to a large extent, both for herself and for those she led to safety. Once she staged a mock funeral procession right through the middle of a Southern town and led all the "mourners" on through town, past the cemetery, and north to safety.

After gaining her freedom, Tubman devoted the entire remainder of her active life to freeing slaves. When not leading blacks out of the South, she worked hard and saved her money. Her activities were financed by money she earned herself, in addition to that donated by Northern abolitionists.

Harriet Tubman lived to the age of ninety-two and is buried in Auburn, New York, where there is a plaque in her honor on the court house.

For obvious reasons, there were no comprehensive records kept on the Underground Railroad, so we cannot be really certain how many whites were involved, but there are records (books, articles, etc.) that prove a great many free blacks and black churches were heavily involved.

One of Tubman's favorite routes to freedom was north from New York City to Albany, then west to Syracuse, Rochester, and across the Niagara Falls into Canada. Slave catchers were not allowed into Canada, and there was no way a disgruntled former slave master could extradite them.

The path along northern New York, starting from Troy and Albany, was dotted with black churches that were ready, willing, and able to assist the escaping slave.

One of those churches is the Israel African Methodist Episcopal Church in Albany, New York. It bears a plaque in the church grounds that reads, "Israel A.M.E., founded in 1828. Oldest Black church in upstate New York. Underground R.R. station during slavery, present church renovated in 1984."

Founded in 1828, the church at the present site was built in 1854. This means it was built four years after the Fugitive Slave Act was passed.

In the spring of 1992, the author visited the Albany A.M.E. Church and met with the minister and members of the congregation. One of the ladies present volunteered that the church had been in another location prior to 1854. As has been pointed out before, no one, North or South, ever foresaw the end of slavery. Undoubtedly, one of the principal functions of the Albany A.M.E. Church in 1854 was that of assisting escaping slaves, so a reasonable assumption is that a new church was built in order to better fulfill this dedication.

During my visit at the Albany church, I inquired about a hidden room or rooms and was met with blank stares. No one seemed to have any information regarding hiding places in the church. While

I was suggesting that, due to the severity of the 1850 Fugitive Slave Act, the first place a federal marshal would look for an escaping slave would be a black church, an elderly woman in the back of the group piped up, "In the back, down under the coal bin; that's where they hid the slaves!"

She went on to explain that her father had been the minister of that church when she was a little girl, and that many times she had heard the fact discussed that the slaves had been hidden below the coal bin.

A cursory search revealed that below a staircase in the rear of the church was a bricked-up area, covered by a wire mesh screen, that was most likely where the coal bin had been. Directly to the left, under the stairs, is a dark, wooden panel that has been secured with white plaster on all four sides. If there is a staircase leading down to hidden rooms, it is most likely behind that panel. There is a metal arm projecting from the wall to the left of the panel. The arm serves no ostensible purpose and may have been placed there to lock and unlock the panel, which probably slides to the left, under the stairwell.

The rear corner of the church, where the back door is located, is extremely canted. This would make it virtually impossible for prying eyes to observe any person, or group of persons, entering or exiting the back door of the church.

Older books about the UGRR state that it shut down upon the advent of the Civil War. According to the people in this study, that statement is definitely not true. The operation changed considerably, there being black passengers exclusively (and maybe spies) early in the war, which gave way primarily to white, escaping Union soldiers, after the slaves were declared free in 1863, and as more and more Yank soldiers found themselves lost behind enemy lines as the war progressed.

REFERENCES

World Book Encyclopedia. Chicago, IL: World Book, 1987.

Long Memory: The Black Experience in America, M. Berry & J. Blassingame. New York: Oxford U. Press, 1982.

Who Built America? New York: David McKay, 1990.

Harriet Tubman, Judith Bentley. Danbury Court, NY: Franklin Watts, 1990.

The Underground Railroad, Charles Blockson. New York: Berkeley, 1989.

The Underground Railroad, Stein. Chicago, IL: Children's Press.

The Underground Railroad: From Slavery to Freedom, Wilbur Siebert. North Stratford, NH: Ayer Co., 1974.

Terry Pompa was born in Rockford, Illinois.
Currently she is a student. She lived in Lake Elsinore
approximately eight years, is the mother of two children,
and has never been to Virginia.
Her role in the story is that of Allie Morgan,
a young girl whose family was deeply involved
in the Underground Railroad activities in Millboro.

CHAPTER SEVEN

ALLIE

TERRY POMPA IS A RESIDENT of Lake Elsinore and a friend of Jo Colliers, whom we will meet later as "Mary Alice."

After stating that she was only eight years old, she announced that she was frightened but uncertain as to why. Her name was Alice, and she had a younger sister and brother. Maybe Morgan was her last name, and her family called her Allie, not Alice.

Moving ahead to the year 1861, we heard that she attended a small school and had to walk around the town to get there, since her mother did not like her going through town. It was full of soldiers, and there were bales and boxes of stuff all around, because it kept coming into town on the train.

The house she lived in was small, with a big yard. There were not a lot of trees around right near her house, because they took the trees away when they built the town.

She felt the town was near a river but professed not to know much about the mill.

"Maybe I haven't been here a long time. Maybe we just moved into town, because I don't feel like I know the town very well. The soldiers are wearing grey uniforms, and the people speak with a southern accent. My family is upset about the war. There's a secret of some kind; maybe that's why I don't know much about the war. They don't tell us kids much, because then we can't tell, if we don't know."

Allie was the oldest, and she went to school whenever her mom did not need her at home.

"School is okay, but it's not my favorite thing."

She was familiar with Mr. Warren, who ran the general store. "He has very sharp features, a big guy. He has a loud voice and talks a lot, mostly about politics. Doesn't like the damn war and is definitely pro-Union. Caused trouble!"

There were a lot of things going on in that town, she observed. "They were smuggling people . . . people? . . . (she laughed in surprise) . . . I helped—they had children. We hid some of them, sometimes in the basement of our house . . . had to keep them quiet. Sometimes you had to take parents away from their children, take them a few at a time—a parent and a child, and there's a parent and child left. *They weren't supposed to bring their children.* But some of them had to, because they didn't want them to be killed. They came in wagons, hidden under the straw, under the packages, in trunks, sometimes in boxes, trunks, or coffins. If the soldiers stopped them, they wouldn't open the coffins, because they thought there were bodies in there. They were marked like they were dead soldiers. Some of them were marked like Union soldiers, so they could be sent back North. We had a basement; it was like the full size of our house. We didn't have a root cellar, like some did. A big basement, not very deep; tall people had to bend over."

Allie's mother was short and pretty, with dark, curly hair. Her father wore an outfit like a uniform, but with no insignia. He had high, shiny boots, no hat, and a gun at his waist.

"He was definitely not a farmer; he was *put* there for the reason of getting those people out. I don't know why he was chosen, but he was sent by the North. He was born in the South and lived in a small town all his life."

Allie knew John, as he was a close friend of her dad's. They may even have been related, perhaps cousins. The two of them got together a lot, to talk over "business," as they called it. They were about the same age.

"A lady was shot a while ago, and now everyone's real nervous." This was one of the women involved in the smuggling ring;

we will hear about her death later. When Becky's name came up, Allie explained, "She was the lady that got raped. She was a nice lady and very pretty. She had a real little boy. I don't think I went to her funeral; I think I was probably at the house putting out food for people. They wouldn't let me go to the funeral, but I felt pain as though I was related to her."

Since Lenette (Sally) and Terry (Allie) both currently live in Las Vegas, it made sense to regress them together, while visiting the Nevada town.

When we started, Sally was six and Allie was nine years old. Sally said that Allie's last name was possibly Johnson, or more likely Morgan. This is interesting, because in an earlier session Allie had declared her name to be Morgan. The two were friends, but Sally was a little in awe of Allie.

"She is taller than me, a year or two older, and I always looked up to her. Tall and thin, and real long hair, past her shoulders, light brown hair, and green eyes, and very pretty. I always wanted to look like her." Allie was surprised and impressed by what Sally said, and it made her feel "pretty special."

When she was asked to describe the larger room under Grandma's house, Sally said the ceiling was made of heavy planks like the smaller room, and that nothing had been put on the wood when it was installed. (Author's note: the wood in the ceiling of the smaller room is very shiny and looks as though it had been lacquered or treated with something.) The larger room is situated about one-and-a-half feet below the earth's surface and was definitely put there before the house was built. "It had to be, as the room extended well beyond the perimeters of the house."

The fireplace in Grandma's house had been made of stone and had a wooden mantle. I instructed Sally to look along under the mantle and see if there is a place where the mortar is gone. When she answered in the affirmative, I inquired what that was used for and was surprised to hear "to hide money." Evidently there was a hole under the mantel where Grandma stashed money.

The speaking hole, she continued, "was over to the right and was about two or three inches long. You could hear them real well when they talked into the tube." The tube below was located to the right of the stairs as one descended and was "hidden behind something, like a drape, and was about three feet up from the ground. It kinda hung down for easy access."

The smaller room, located under the shed, was more of a service or utility room, used for instance to stash bodies when someone died. A small alcove was situated off the room, which was a toilet area—they had the chamber pots in there, or possibly a privy arrangement of some type.

Sally proceeded to describe the tunnel that connected the two rooms. "It is long and skinny, about five or six feet long, and you had to crawl through it. I never went through that tunnel—almost did once, but I got scared. It is not concrete; that's why I was scared. More like dirt, real rounded, hardly any light."

When asked whether there were ever any Confederate deserters hidden in these underground rooms, Allie answered quickly, "No, Poppa wouldn't allow it. They came, but Poppa said no. There were white men in tattered clothes, but not Confederate, because we would be afraid they would turn us in." Sally added that she had seen soldiers, but only in Union blue.

The fact was mentioned that there are still a large number of old bottles, presumably liquor bottles, in that smaller room, and we heard from Sally that "they were for medicinal purposes. Some of the Negroes—and I remember soldiers in blue uniforms down there, hurt, and some of the black people were sick too." Sally stated that Grandma had been pretty tight with the people in the church near her house, and one of the men in the congregation used to bring the booze to her. Allie picked up the story, "He had a beard, and he brought it in a wagon. The wagon was full of jugs and bottles, and they were covered with wicker and stored in wooden cases. He made the booze, and he made the cases too." Sally nodded affirmation.

About the church that stands near where Grandma's house was, Sally declared adamantly that the one now there was not the one Grandma attended. The older one was made of stone, dull gray stone, maybe river rock, and had darker gray mortar between the stones. This older church is very apparent in the picture I was given of 1800s Millboro. Since *Mission to Millboro* was published, several people have claimed that the photograph was made in the late 1800s or early 1900s. However, the white clapboard church that stands in the spot was dedicated in 1882; therefore, the old picture of the town, because it clearly shows the older church, has to predate 1882.

When asked how many houses in town hid slaves, Sally said, "I think three or four." There was one quite near to Grandma's house, and Allie's house was farther out, on the edge of town, pretty much by itself.

Several people have mentioned the large, two-story stone house, the one mentioned as being near to Grandma's, which was located just off the upper right corner of the old photo of the town. Honey had described it as a big, two-story house on a large lot. The front door was in the center of the house, and, after entering, one turned right, went down a hallway, and under the bedroom in the corner of the house was the large, hidden room. The floor slid under one of the beds to give quick access, but most people went through the trap door that lifted up in the closet, exposing a wooden ladder.

Sally described the entrance located under the bed: "It's long; they pull it out; there's no lifting; it's on the same level. You know how a closet door opens up? It slides on a trolley. You can't leave it open, otherwise people will know. They just crawl under the bed, because the bed was high. Only skinny people could go down into the room that way." The more conventional way was through the trap door in the long, narrow closet. There was a rope lying on the floor of the closet that one merely picked up and pulled. No attempt was made to conceal the rope; the owners just kept shoes and clothing over it. She ended her discourse by stating that the house was about six or eight blocks from Grandma's house, that it stood pretty much by itself, and that there was a vacant corner lot next to it. (Today the lot where the stone house once stood is vacant, and the corner lot next to it holds a house.)

The room that was hidden under Allie's house was entered through the living room or parlor. One moved out the rug, lifted out a whole section of the floor, a false furnace grate, and descended a stone staircase that ran along a wall. The roof of the hidden room was made of the customary wooden planks and the floor was dirt. Allie was vague about how the refugees entered and left the room, but Sally explained that there were tunnels going left and right. The one that went to the left (as she was viewing it) was a small, skinny tunnel that probably led to Robin's Nest, and the other tunnel led off towards town, linking up with the network of tunnels under the town, all of which eventually led to the Presbyterian Church above Grandma's house.

Allie's family's (the Morgan's) house was located a long way out of town, out near Rose's bawdy house. That would explain how the tunnel led up to Robin's Nest. It was a white, one-and-a-half story, loft-type frame house, which Allie claims was up a hill, far back off the road, back behind the whorehouse. Samuel, however, later stated adamantly that the place was next to Rose's brothel but situated directly on the road.

Allie volunteered the following information: "There were certain houses that only accepted adults, and there were one or two where children could go in. They separated them." One can only guess at how much truth this statement contains.

CHAPTER EIGHT

MARY ALICE

JO COLLIER IS A FORMER CITY EMPLOYEE of Lake Elsinore. She was identified by a couple of people in the story as having lived in Millboro during the Civil War.

She was in her twenties when we first met her under hypnosis. Unmarried, she lived at home with her parents, on the farm where she worked from sunup to sundown.

Skipping ahead in time to 1862, she was no longer on the farm, but married and living in town—another town, just a little larger than the one near the farm. She lived in a nice house on the edge of town and was happy in her marriage, especially because she did not have to work nearly as hard as she had on the farm, and her husband was a pretty nice guy. This town is much busier than the previous one, with the train bringing in barrels, crates, and boxes, on a regular basis, and men in grey uniforms all over the place.

Jo said that her name back in that lifetime was Mary Alice, but that her husband called her Alice, because his mother's name was Mary.

Her husband, she said, kept a store of some type, across the street and down a ways from the feed store.

"He always puts on a suit to go to work, but he's not a banker. He's a tall man, and I feel that he's got to do with . . . nails . . . somehow . . . construction . . . and I feel his name is Henry. I was like, well, not very well educated, and I felt really lucky to get married, because there were not any eligible men where I was. We

Jo Collier was born in Artesia, California.
Her profession is in a finance-related field.
She lived in Lake Elsinore for ten years.
She has one grown son.
Jo has driven through Virginia once,
when she stopped briefly in Norfolk.
Her role in the story is that of Mary Alice,
who was married to Henry Wilson,
the undertaker in Millboro.

met in church; he was in the town near our farm on business. We knew each other only a short time before we married. My husband was a good man, a very stern person. I knew he knew a lot of what was going on, but he didn't say a thing. He expected me to stay home and take care of the house. He was not a big socializer, but I have a feeling that he knew *everybody* in town."

She was asked if the name Wilson sounded familiar, and she looked stunned.

"I can see him so plainly—a tall, stern fellow; thin; bowler hat. His suit was black, and his vest was black with grey stripes in it. He had a . . . hawk nose. He works in lumber but is always dressed up."

We knew exactly who he was, and her description of Henry Wilson was exactly as he has been pictured by others in the group. Jo left the first session very puzzled and, after about one half hour, she called up to say, "He was the undertaker in town; that's why he was dressed up but dealt in lumber and nails."

She was absolutely right. Later, she elaborated, "He is an undertaker. Sometimes he builds coffins, but most of the time he has a worker do it. He drove a lorry and was a big factor in the UGRR, hauling Negroes and soldiers in and out of town in his wagon. He would put them in coffins, nail down the lids, and the guards never challenged him. He looked like Abe Lincoln, but was a little bit heavier. A commanding stature, very uncommunicative. He was stern, but not nearly as stern as he looked. I was very sheltered and naive, and he kept me that way. All that was expected of me was to cook a lot of food sometimes, and people would sneak in late at night and eat it. Henry did more than smuggle people. He was involved in a lot of stuff; I wasn't sure how much, but he knew exactly what was going on in that town, and he was making money; he was being paid by the North. One time he left town for a long time, and I heard later he had gone west, maybe to New Mexico, and brought back a wagonload of gold. If that was true, I never saw it."

She knew Alice, or Allie, but not well, because Allie was just a little girl. Allie had a little brother about the same age as Mary

Alice's son. Mary Alice lived "away from the train, over near the river and the mill." In those days, it was called Old Millboro, but today it is referred to as Millboro Springs. She knew Allie's mother quite well. "Henry went over there a lot; they were involved in the ring, too. Their name was . . . Morgan. I never saw the Negroes or soldiers in their house, but I know that her (Allie's) mom would always be . . . afraid. Sometimes she would come over just to get out of the house. She would come over and we would have tea. Her name, I think, was Jane. I didn't know her too well, but it was as if the people knew that the only place to go when you got scared was to others who were involved too. They are the only ones you dared talk to."

Evidently, the UGRR group limited their socializing to within the clan. Mary Alice told of going out to the Green Valley Farm one time.

"We went to a party at the Lewis house on the Green Valley Farm. We didn't see the whole house, but I remember a large foyer. It was a dinner party, then afterwards, they moved some tables and chairs to make room for dancing. It was a big room, with highly waxed hardwood floors, beautiful. I never went into the basement, did not know exactly what went on down there, but they were involved—that I do know. There was a river that ran behind that house, quite a distance behind. Mostly we socialized only with people who were involved, and you were very careful if other people were around. Mr. Lewis and his wife were older than the rest of us; they both had white hair.

CHAPTER NINE

THE WEDDING

ABOUT SIX MONTHS AFTER *Mission to Millboro* was published, I received a package from a man in Warm Springs, Virginia. In it was a copy of an application for a marriage license dated December 9, 1858, for Andrew A. Ailstock and Mary Jane Ailstock; a copy of the actual marriage license, and a page of genealogical records concerning the marriage applicants. Both were twenty-one years of age, and both lived in Bath County. The husband's mother was Nancy Ailstock, who had never married, and the bride's mother was listed as Liza Ailstock, who likewise had never married. Andrew was obviously illiterate, as he had signed the application with an X. The marriage was solemnized by Reverend San Brown.

Although I knew that there were two Andrew Ailstocks in Millboro at this time, my initial reaction was that this might be John and Becky's marriage license, but after studying the papers a while, it became abundantly clear that this was another couple. The date alone was wrong, as John and Becky had been married several years already and had four children when this wedding occurred. Also, our John (or Andrew) had a good primary education and was well able to sign his name.

Telling Becky that the date was December 9 and the year was 1858, I asked her where she was and what was going on. Expecting her to exuberantly describe the festivities to me, it was a surprise that she became very quiet; I could hardly get her to speak, which was a whole new demeanor for the usually gregarious Becky.

Picture of Rev. Sam Brown, from the
History of Windy Cove Presbyterian Church,
Millboro Springs, Virginia. 1749-1929.

To the Clerk of the *County Court* Court of
Bath County in the State of Virginia.

] HEREBY CERTIFY, That the following is a correct Statement of a **Marriage** solemnized by me in the County aforesaid:

Date of Marriage, = *December 9th 1858.*

Place of Marriage, *Millero Depot. Bath Co. Va.*

Full Names of Parties married, *Andrew Ailstock & Mary Jane Ailstock*

Age of Husband, = *21 years.*

Age of Wife, = *21 years.*

Condition of Husband, (widowed or single,) *Single*

Condition of Wife, (widowed or single,) *Single*

Place of Husband's Birth, = *Rockbridge Co. Va.*

Place of Wife's Birth, = *Alleghaney Co, Va*

Place of Husband's Residence, = *Bath Co. Va*

Place of Wife's Residence, — *Bath Co. Va.*

Names of Husband's Parents, = *Nancy Ailstock = {she was never married*

Names of Wife's Parents, = *Eliza Ailstock = {she was never married*

Occupation of Husband, = *Farmer*

Given under my hand as a
(legally authorized to solemnize Marriages,) this *9th*
day of *December* A. D. 185 *8*

Sam. Brown

☞ The Clerks of the County Courts will furnish Ministers and others with these Blanks when they may need them.

☞ This Certificate must be returned to the Clerk's office by the person performing the marriage ceremony, within two months after the marriage.

Marriage license issued to Mary Jane and Andrew Ailstock,
signed by Sam Brown.

Payton Reynolds Ailstock

Payton Ailstock (1/2/1860-9/28/1929) was born near Millboro, the son of Andrew A. and Mary Jane Ailstock.

Payton was married three times, first to Mary Elizabeth Matheny, who died January 23, 1903, and is buried in Lone Star Cemetery. Their children were: Sarah Frances (Bridgette) (1882-5/2/1929); Henry Pole (4/26/1884-4/14/1964); Jesse, (no record of birth or death); Bessie Maude (Dudley), died 11/7/1906; Mattie Sarah (Bocook) (3/2/1887-4/10/1927); Elsie Lee (Thomas) (2/26/1898-11/2/1968); and a baby boy who died in infancy.

Payton's second wife was Julia Wright Garber, who died in 1910 and is buried in Mount Pleasant Cemetery at Falling Springs. Their children were: Irene Margaret (Riley Sparks) (10/30/1906-1/1/1937); a baby girl, who died in infancy; and Robert Edward Lee (3/24/1910-6/21/1989).

Payton married his third wife, Mary Elizabeth Armentrout (6/28/1893-7/28/1919) on December 27, 1910. Both she and Payton are buried in Mt. Hope Cemetery near Hot Springs. By this marriage were the following children: Gordon Thomas (4/17/1912-11/24/1988); Annie Laura (2/22/1915-); Leonard Lance (8/23/1916-9/8/1943), killed in World War II; and Thelma Lillian (5/2/1919-5/11/1919). I am the last living child of Payton Ailstock of the 14 children by his three wives.

Payton moved his family from the Thomas Place in 1917 to the McClintic house on Jackson River, where he was a share-crop farmer for the Revercomb and Fudge families until 1926. This was a beautiful old brick home, built in 1774. It was torn down and all this farm is now covered by Lake Moomaw. *Submitted by Annie A. Lowry.*

Payton R. and Mary Elizabeth
Armentrout Ailstock.

Biography of Peyton Ailstock, son of Andrew and Mary Jane, whose wedding Becky described to us.

Maureen Williamson was born in Boston, Massachusetts.
The mother of four children, she is currently occupied
with the role of homemaker and busily raising
her four-year-old daughter.
She has lived in the Elsinore area for eighteen years.
Maureen had not been to Virginia prior to this research,
but has been to Millboro twice since.
Her role in the story is that of Becky, a central figure
in the Millboro drama, whose life is chronicled in detail in
the previous book, Mission to Millboro.
It was Maureen's memories of Becky that triggered
the entire Millboro saga.

Finally, she admitted that she was in town, and it was early afternoon. There were a lot of people milling about; they were all dressed up in their church clothes. She was outside, near Honey's boarding house. The impression conveyed was that she was definitely not happy about something. John and the kids were with her, she admitted, and there was a ceremony of some sort taking place, but she "didn't want to talk about it!" A few moments passed and she said, "I think it is happy—think there is some reason why I don't want to talk about it."

She stated that she was already married and had been for about ten years. "I don't know why I am getting married when I am already married." Looking thoroughly confused, she continued, "It's John's cousin—it's somebody else getting married."

Was she upset about the marriage? "Well, I'll tell you, it seems like they shouldn't be getting married. Their names are John and Mary Jane. There's something shameful about them both, and that's why they are getting married. . . . It seems to me it's something that shouldn't be happening."

While she was discussing the event, she related that she was standing on the steps of the boarding house. The marriage took place in a private house on the other side of the corral. She continued that the happy couple might have been cousins or even brother and sister, even though they had separate mothers. It was obvious that Becky adamantly disapproved of this union, and she added, as an afterthought, "They don't have *any* money!"

Were she and John part of the ceremony? Becky became very agitated over that question and said, somewhat confidentially, "Well, you see, I have to keep quiet about all that; it could be an embarrassment. Everybody in town knows they are both illegitimate, but we are not supposed to talk about it. Both mothers are here, and they are very happy about events. There will be a small party afterwards." It was suggested to Becky that perhaps the marriage was in a private home rather than a church, because the bride and groom were both illegitimate. She answered, "I don't know; I just know they will be having simpletons!"

Becky's response to this marriage was totally unexpected. Being the party girl that she was, it was thought that she would have thrown herself into the festivities.

Coming up out of the trance, Maureen, in the conscious state, was very agitated. "That was a shame. That marriage should never have taken place. Becky could not understand, for the life of her, why these two were getting married."

The newlyweds had a baby boy, about a year after the wedding, named Payton. A picture of Payton was enclosed in the material sent to me. Payton is dressed like a farmer of the time. His appearance does not suggest that he had the IQ of a rocket scientist. Whether or not he was a simpleton is a matter for speculation.

Looking at the photo of Payton, Maureen laughed loudly and continued, "Those two were closely related; it was a sacrilege for them to get married. It's possible they were brother and sister. They probably had the same father. There was something I was taking really personally about it, and I think it was that they had the same names as John and myself; also everyone knew he was related to John."

Maureen ended her discourse by stating, "I got into *more trouble* for talking about that union, did I ever!" She could not tell me what the trouble was about and suggested cryptically, "You'll have to ask Becky."

So ask Becky we did, at a later date. The bride and groom looked a great deal alike and were brother and sister. Their mothers were sisters, and they shared a common father. He was a local unmarried man, and Becky did not know him very well. "He is pretty old, and I think his name is Edward. He lives in town on the other side of Old Snake Road. He builds chimneys, is really not that much of a lady's man."

She continued to express her outrage over the situation. "When the preacher says does someone have objections, well, there are objections. Their children, if they have any, will be simpletons! It's not lawful. John says if you help somebody to break the law, then you are breaking the law too, and I don't think I want to break the law. Besides, if he didn't want to know, then why did he ask?" This last question she literally spit out.

In a flash, it dawned on me how Becky had managed to get into so much trouble over this marriage, and I queried, "Are you thinking about standing up and saying that you object to the wedding?" Becky shot back (getting worked up again, evidently taking the entire matter very seriously), "I thought about it before I did it; you have to think everything through before you do it. And then John just doesn't understand. If the preachers says, do you have objections to it, you have to stand up and tell the truth. He said, 'Be there anyone present who can show reason why these two should not be joined in holy matrimony, let him speak now or forever hold his peace.' I stood up and said that it's not lawful, because they are kin, and I think that they have the same daddy and that their babies will be simpletons. John said that there's some things that I don't understand, and I just have to let it go. After I stood up and announced that I objected to the wedding, the preacher didn't say nothing to me; he said to John that I should sit down and be quiet and keep my peace."

Several others told Becky to sit down and keep her peace also, but she totally ignored them all. Later she said that her arm was about two inches longer from John pulling on it, trying to get her to sit down. The wedding eventually continued, despite Becky's objections. She maintained that in the eyes of God, this was not a civilized thing.

Mary Jane died young, according to Becky. "I think he might have whopped her upside the head. He whacked her in town one time, I saw him, whacked her with his hand. He was a farmer, and neither of them had any schooling. I think he is a really lucky man if he can manage to drive his wagon!" Sarcasm dripped from every word.

When conscious, Maureen stated that the two women involved were not too bright, and that the man who had fathered the children did not really have too much to offer; he was just there and available. Becky had stood up at the wedding and objected, loud and clear! It was a big scandal in town. She felt it was ridiculous for the minister to ask if anyone objected, when he really didn't care. John was a prominent man in town and was quite upset by the entire fracas. The preacher would not talk to Becky; he just kept exhorting John to control his wife. Meanwhile, Becky continued to berate the minister, totally deaf to all around her, while waiting for the minister to answer her. John was furious, and they fought about it for months afterward. Why did the preacher ask if anybody objected, if he did not want to know, and why would the preacher not talk to *her?* Becky and Constance were the avant garde of women's liberation in the Millboro area, because in those days a woman was a man's property. Samuel claims that the "Becky" incident was discussed and laughed over throughout Bath County. It was all anyone talked about for months. He even wrote about it in his newsletter.

Later, when Maureen, Smokey, and I were in Millboro, we were loaned a Presbyterian Church book. Thumbing through it, Maureen gave a loud squeal when she came across the picture of a certain minister. I checked it out and, sure enough, it was Samuel Brown, the same man she had tangled with at the wedding. From Reverend Brown's photo, he looks as though he might have founded the hellfire, brimstone, and damnation school of ministry. Maureen said that John was scared of few men, but that Reverend Brown intimidated him thoroughly.

John claims that he was not nearly as angry as he pretended to be—embarrassed, yes, but the anger was a front. Underneath it all, he was really rather amused at Becky's temerity in challenging the preacher. According to John, a large part of why Becky was so incensed was because she believed the other Andrew was really John's cousin and considered his actions an affront to the entire Ailstock family. He, of course, knew that the man was no blood relation of his, and he was able to remain fairly objective about what was transpiring. At that time, Becky did not know that John was not an Ailstock. It was shortly after this wedding that he dropped that bomb on her.

As we will discover later, John admitted that he told Becky that he was three-quarters Indian at his mother's insistence. Her reasoning, according to Becky, was that Liz wanted them all to move to California. Somehow she got it into her head that there was no discrimination out there, and that she and Little Eagle could openly live together out West. She figured that if Becky knew about John's Indian background, and that they (Becky and John) were not legally married, Becky would agree to move. If John and his family all agreed to the migration, then Little Eagle would pretty much have to come along.

Grandma Liz had not anticipated that this shock to Becky would precipitate the unraveling of the marriage. Evidently, she failed to understand just how racist Becky was.

Once, when discussing the war, Becky stated with feeling, "It is just awful for these boys to be dying for them slaves. Those niggers have it good—food, clothes, and they don't want to be free!" She did not give too much thought to the pros and cons of the war. We suspect deep thinking was not her long suit, but she resented what the war was doing to her quality of life.

John was constantly giving her lectures about the "greater good." She said, "I have no lamp oil, no flour, no food, no apples, sugar—life is no fun at all." Trying to feed her children was becoming a virtual impossibility. All her livestock had been stolen, and at one time she tried to hide some of her chickens—and we all know how easy it is to hide chickens!

CHAPTER TEN

ELIZABETH OF GREEN VALLEY FARM

WHEN SHARON OLIVE FIRST CAME FROM Texas to be hypnotized for *Mission to Millboro,* we were unable to discover a name for her. However, early into her second hypnosis, she readily came up with the name Elizabeth. She is the third Elizabeth to appear in the Millboro story. First was Liz (Barbara Roberts), who was John's mother. Then there was Elizabeth (Diana Lovegren), John and Becky's youngest daughter, and now came Sharon's Elizabeth of Green Valley Farm.

When Elizabeth arrived at the old plantation house in Green Valley during the Civil War, it was not in good shape. There were weeds all over the place. She could see herself being driven up the driveway in a buckboard rig. Tired after a long trip, it was good to see the older, white-haired man waiting to greet her outside the house. Although she was only in her early thirties, her body ached all over from the long days of traveling and the jostling of the wagon.

Elizabeth had not met the man before—he was somehow related to her dead husband. That he was overjoyed to see her, though, was very obvious. Kind, thoughtful, and gracious, he was moved to tears by her coming. There was almost no one else around. His wife, who had long been bedridden, had died awhile back, and except for a handful of slaves, he was there all alone and desperately

81

*The exterior of Green Valley Farm as it looks today.
The wooden door below the brick chimney leads down
into a small basement.*

*One can clearly see in the photo the old staircase leading down
from the kitchen area. It has been filled in with mortar.*

*This old wall, about five inches behind the brick wall,
can be seen, where bricks have fallen away.*

Sharon Olive was born in Mankato, Minnesota, in 1943.
Currently living in Texas, she is divorced and
has two children and one grandchild.
Sharon has never been to Virginia and had not heard of
Millboro until this study. Her role in the story is
as Elizabeth of Green Valley Farm.

needed someone to help him to run the plantation and the work in progress below the house.

No one, neither John, Ruthie, nor Elizabeth, has been able to be certain about the old man's name, but Mary Alice (Jo Collier) referred to him as "Mr. Lewis"—and he apparently liked to be called by a title that designated military rank, Captain, or perhaps Colonel.

"The Colonel" was a very dapper man. "He dresses very elegantly. Every day it's the same routine, like a ritual. He had one of those hats . . . he was still very good looking. The hat was a beaver hat with a felt band, a big brim, grey. He was impeccable. The hat looked very good on him. Everything he had was very expensive, but a lot of stuff was not there. He had a beautiful ring, had it in a vault someplace, not on the plantation. In fact, most of their money was out of the country, maybe up North. That's how they maintained their wealth; they took things out of there. They were hauling things out of there when this thing broke; even before it broke, they started getting things out of there, antiques, jewelry. This was even years before the war—like they all knew. They were in business and could feel, even smell, the war coming."

We asked Elizabeth if she had planned the trip to Virginia for a long time and heard, "Well, they had to do something with me. There was a . . . stigma? . . . And I had to get away. The family helped me to get away, and they thought I would be a lot of help to the old man."

When asked if it was her marriage that had brought about her troubles, she replied, "I am getting chills; yes, I think it was something to do with it. It was my husband; there was something wrong there. The family was very nice . . . some sort of scandal. I am getting chills; yes, they thought I would be better off out of there. There wasn't much left . . . they were very concerned for me."

The subject of children came up and we heard, "My God, the children!"

There had been two children, a boy and a girl. Because she was getting very upset, she was instructed to view it from a distance, unemotionally.

"They separated us. They took the children, because they wanted to keep them close to the family. My husband died . . . they took the children because my husband was in a scandal." Later, in the conscious state, she was able to sort the whole thing out.

"They didn't tell me very much about the scandal, other than that he was killed. Initially I was told that he was killed in the war, but something came out to the effect that I must save my children, so that they could lead a normal life. That was what the deal was. They were very kind. My first husband's family took the children. My first husband was the father of the children, and he was the war hero; he died in the war. My second husband's family didn't know me very well . . . and he wasn't really very happy with me. The scandal was that he was shot by his brother . . . he really married me on the rebound, which I didn't know. He loved his brother's wife, had wanted to marry her. The whole thing went back to the mother; he was forever competing for her attention, which she always gave to his oldest brother. There was continually big competition between the brothers. He left me to do the war thing and discovered that his brother was not at the plantation. He found out where his brother's regiment was and, knowing his sister-in-law would be at the plantation, he went there and told her that her husband had been killed; then he finessed her into bed. Right at this time, his brother came in, who hadn't been killed at all, found his brother and his wife in bed together, and shot and killed them both."

Elizabeth felt as though she was a jinx and said she did not want to become involved with anyone again in her entire life, that she was the kiss of death! It was a terrible time in her life. Both her husbands' families were very concerned about her, and they decided that to tone down the scandal it would be best for the kids to go to their father's family and for her to go to Millboro (or Green Valley Farm). The families were extremely wealthy, definitely upper crust, and their networking was very intense.

"They wouldn't dare let that money get out of the family. I wasn't really all that wealthy, but my first husband was a big hero, an officer in the Confederacy. I don't know why my second husband married me; he didn't have much to do with my kids. He was not around very much, but I think he wanted to have a baby very badly. His family was wonderful to me; they even sent money to take care of my children, and they weren't even of their family."

There had been another girl in that house, one who had lived there before Elizabeth arrived. Her name was Ruthie, and today she is Jackie Spagnolo. Ruthie's story was told in *Mission to Millboro.* Constance's mother, Ava, was Ruthie's aunt, and when she was orphaned, she went to live with her Aunt Ava. This precipitated an impossible situation, as Constance was unwilling to accept her attractive cousin and caused a lot of trouble. The upshot was that Ruthie was adopted to the elderly couple who owned the old plantation house. They were childless and very happy to give the little girl a home.

Elizabeth and Ruthie had never met, but when Ruthie's name was mentioned, Elizabeth gasped and exclaimed, "There's a picture of her; oh yes, she is beautiful! It is an oil painting, beautiful. The old man's face lit up when he looked at that portrait. I got the feeling . . . I think there was something going on between the old man and the young girl. Nothing was ever really said, but there were hints. He didn't talk much, but he frequently looked at the picture fondly, and from the look on his face, I thought it was more than a paternal fondness. I don't think the wife ever knew. The feeling I had was that she loved her husband dearly and loved Ruthie, and never suspected a thing. I felt very safe with him; he was kind to me, acted like a father, and I needed that. He was just so happy to have me there . . . there was so much going on, and (in a lower voice) it was really scary what was going on there."

She continued, "It's what's going on under the house that is scary; we are all going to get killed over that deal."

Many times throughout her narrative she reiterated the fact that they would probably all be killed over activities taking place in the basement—shot, preemptively, for treason, without benefit of judge or jury.

Discussing the conditions below the house, she mentioned there was a lot of "river rock." The term *river rock* has come up many times in conversations with the Millboro people, and we can only assume that it was a type of rock found near the river and under the ground locally that was used a lot in building.

"It smells, and it's damp. They have slop buckets, but many of them just urinate along the walls. The men, they were hurting and they were scared. It was awful down there; it smelled musty, like there was a lot of water around. It wasn't like the cellar, the storm cellar where we kept the potatoes and things—that was fairly dry. This room is hidden. In the main room, you can't tell anything. They are off the main room; there is more than one room down in that basement. I'm not sure the rooms are even connected—it is not directly under the house, it is away. The smell, I can't believe those guys; they have no place to go, and there are smells of gangrene. Some of the men are wounded, and the smell is awful!"

Next to being apprehended by the Confederates, about the worst scenario to occur for one of those brave souls operating the UGRR was to have an escapee die while down below. Deaths presented a myriad of problems. The corpse had to be disposed of immediately, particularly in the warm weather. Of course, in the summer, the problem was more easily solved, as around the plantation house in Green Valley there were many acres of land in which to bury the corpse. The cold weather presented a more serious problem, as the ground was hard and difficult to turn over. Always there was the problem of prying eyes.

Elizabeth continued, "They smuggled the bodies out with the rest of the men; there was a community grave somewhere nearby. They didn't dare put a body in the creek. . . . (Very quietly, with a look of sheer horror) sometimes, if they were recently dead and had died of wounds and were free of disease, they . . . *butchered* them . . . for food. There was a regular slaughter barn somewhere nearby; that's where it was done. If the bodies were rotting or had lain around for awhile, they would not use them. Usually there were between thirty and forty people down there, sometimes less."

This horrifying revelation opens a lot of avenues for thought. One must consider the overwhelming responsibility the operators of the UGRR took upon themselves when they became involved in the smuggling. Prior to the Civil War, when only Negroes were the passengers and food was plentiful, things ran smoothly. Elizabeth claimed the "networking" among participants was honed to a fine point—not an easy task in the days before the telephone or radio.

Then came the Civil War, and at first larger numbers of Negroes, anxious to flee for fear that the South might win the war and that their escape route would be closed forever. Then, as the battles in Virginia progressed, and more and more Union soldiers were lost behind enemy lines and escaped from Confederate prisons, the UGRR lines became clogged with both slaves and Yank soldiers frantic to get out of the South. In January 1863, President Lincoln signed the Emancipation Proclamation, setting the blacks free, and the urgency of their situation was eased. The numbers of escaping soldiers increased, however, and this added fuel to a fire fraught with danger.

Slavery in this country dates back to the 1600s. By 1670, law and custom defined all Africans in the colonies as slaves, unless they could prove otherwise. The New England Confederation (1643-1684) was formed partly to strengthen cooperation in returning runaway slaves to their owners. In 1793, Congress passed a weak fugitive slave act that proved difficult to enforce.

It was the Fugitive Slave Act of 1850 that brought the issue to a head. The penalties for aiding or abetting a runaway slave were a fine of one thousand dollars, six months in jail, and civil damages in the amount of one thousand dollars, payable to the slave owner. The financial penalties inflicted were enough to ruin the average citizen, and this drove many out of the UGRR. However, it had the opposite effect with most, particularly in the North. The question arose, "If the slaves were as well treated as the plantation owners insisted they were, if they were well fed, well clothed, and well cared for, why were they defecting by the thousands via the UGRR?

The UGRR was carried on secretly, informally, and at great risk to the participants, who were predominantly Quakers, Presbyterians, and Congregationalists. After the war got under way and their principal cargo became escaping enemy soldiers, this threw a whole new light on what they were doing. What they were doing was treason by anyone's interpretation, and the penalty was death, usually instantaneously and on the spot. If a slave were to die while en route, his body could be fairly easily hidden, and even if the body was discovered, there could be many various reasons why it was where it was found. To have a Union soldier's body lying about was much more incriminating and would be nearly impossible to explain.

Hideous as it seems, cannibalism was a very convenient answer. In the first place, it neatly disposed of the body, except for a few, small, inedible parts, which were easily dispatched, and it solved a much more pressing problem—that of supplying food to the thirty or forty people hidden under the house.

Anyone familiar with the Civil War appreciates that starvation and lack of ammunition were the two salient points that became the final undoing of the Confederacy. From the time in 1864 when Sheridan and Custer's troops torched the entire Shenandoah Valley, there was no food for anyone, anywhere. The operators of the UGRR had little or no food to feed their own families, never mind the terrified, hungry mouths hiding in their basements.

What many fail to realize is that the UGRR was not a matter of delivering a load of escaping souls one day, only to have another operator pick them up the next. Sometimes those people stayed below ground for weeks, even months, until circumstances were such that it was safe to move them on. The weather had to be considered, the proximity of lawmen or enemy troops, and the availability of space and supplies at the next stop. Many factors played into the operation of this freedom movement. High on the list of operator's fears was one or more of the escapees dying while in his care. The problems presented were overwhelming, and his prayer was that they remain quiet and healthy. In order for this to happen, they *had* to be fed and their needs met. To people in this predicament, the matter of cannibalism was merely the ends justifying the means.

"I didn't go down there that much. When I did go, it was usually because the old man wanted me to do something special, like deliver medicine. The smoke hurt my eyes. There was no heat in the basement, and even tho' they weren't supposed to, the men built little fires. When I went in there, I had to pull something aside, like a curtain. It was dirty, and it always hit me on the head. I hated it!"

The outside entrance was seldom used; mostly they went down stone steps that led from a pantry next to the kitchen upstairs and ran along the outer wall of the house. These steps terminated in the small outer room, then anyone who entered had to go in through an arch-like door that opened into the larger basement room.

"The men were brought in, in the dead of night. They were brought in, in wagons, boats, and sometimes they walked—however they could get there. Sometimes the wounded were carried by their buddies, and there was always one 'lead dog' who had either been there before or who knew exactly where to go. They went out through the tunnel and knew that they would be safe within a day or so of leaving the house."

Green Valley is not much more than a day or so's wagon trip from West Virginia, which in 1863 was admitted to the Union.

"They started out in a boat, then somewhere along the line they transferred into a wagon. One time they had this huge thing like a supply train, and there were a lot of Union soldiers hidden in there. A wagon supply train, carrying Confederate supplies. It seemed pretty safe; I couldn't see where in the world they had them hidden. There was ammo and food on the train, and boxes for medications. I think the medication boxes were empty, and I remember thinking, how in the hell did they get them in there?"

Elizabeth recognized pictures of the old Green Valley Farm and stated, as everyone else had, that the pillars back in the 1800s were larger than those on the porch today. She said that John visited periodically; he and the old man always had a lot to talk about. Whenever he did come, he brought medical supplies and food for the people in the basement.

Occasionally, Indians would come and work on the plantation for awhile.

"We all felt so sorry for them; they were hungry. Anybody that was alive in those days was starving. No one was ever turned away. We tried to feed them and give them what we could. The old man was so nice to me; he just opened his arms to me and treated me like a daughter. I did a lot of work up there, and he appreciated it. Awhile after the war, I left the plantation, as things were starting to come back."

CHAPTER 11

RUTHIE

AFTER THE DISCUSSION WITH Elizabeth of Green Valley Farm, it was necessary again to interview Ruthie (Jackie Spagnolo). The idea that she had fled the old plantation house for the bawdy house because of the smuggling activities in the basement had always been there, but the sexual harassment she endured from the old man was a new possibility. She started right out talking about it with no prompting.

"They were an older couple, probably in their fifties, with no children of their own. It was obvious they were very happy to have me, but he . . . (in a hushed voice) . . . was a dirty old man!"

She was very young, in her mid-teens, when she realized he was in love with her.

"He was always after me. He repulsed me. The old woman was in bed most of the time, and she never knew what was going on. There were others who knew or suspected. A few of the people around there knew he was after me. The first time, he just grabbed me, started kissing me in the living room of the house, downstairs, just the two of us. I let him know I did not like it, and after awhile he apologized, but he never believed me. He kept it up, figured I was a young girl and fair game. It was a bad thing, because of his wife and all the people that knew about it. He came into my bedroom many, many times, late at night. It surprised me terribly the first time he showed up; it worried me, scared me, but what could I do? I was always just a little bit afraid of him. There were

Jackie Spagnolo was born in Winchester, Virginia, in 1930.
Her family left Winchester in 1932, and she worked
for many years at Disneyland, in Anaheim, California.
Now retired, she has four children and has lived in
the Elsinore area for twelve years.
She does not know if she has ever been to Millboro.
Her role in the story is that of Ruthie, who lived for a while
at Green Valley Farm and later at Rose's Bawdy House,
as described previously in Mission to Millboro.

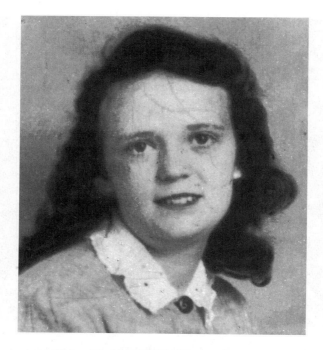

*This old photo of Jackie she claims is
very similar to the portrait of Ruthie that hung
over the mantel in the Green Valley Farm
plantation house. The hair in this picture
has been darkened in order to add to
the resemblance.*

countless times, I can't tell you how many. This had a lot to do with me leaving and going to the bawdy house. I had to get out of there, and I had no place to go. There was no one to help me, no one to talk to. I could not talk to Aunt Ava about it. You don't talk about those kind of things."

The portrait was painted when she was about sixteen or seventeen. It was a very large picture and took a long time to paint. Jackie gave me a photo of herself taken when she was fifteen. She said it looked very much like the portrait of Ruthie except that Ruthie had very dark hair. Actually it was reddish auburn hair, like her Aunt Ava's. Her eyes were a bluish-grey, like Jackie's today. Big eyes, beautiful skin. In the conscious state, Jackie explained, "She was a good, Christian girl and was terribly offended at him chasing her the way he did, with his wife right there in the house. He never abused her, never beat or deprived her, he just pushed it all the time. He was desperately in love with her, but that did not justify his actions. Ruthie worried constantly about getting pregnant, but it was never brought up. He just didn't talk about it."

She spent most of her youth in that house; it was a great big place. Ruthie had been adopted by the older couple when it became inconvenient for her to remain with her Aunt Ava. Her mother had been Ava's sister, and upon her mother's death Ava had taken Ruthie to raise.

Because Constance, selfish and territorial, had bitterly resented having another young, prettier girl invade her arena, she raised such a fuss that finally, in desperation, her mother had decided to find the girl another home.

All had been well when Ruthie was a child, but when she grew into lovely young womanhood, suddenly her stepfather found it impossible to keep his hands off of her.

Obviously, this eventually forced the young girl to escape to the sanctuary of the bawdy house. If she was going to be raped every night, at least she would be paid for it and given a certain amount of freedom.

The old man was frantic when he discovered Ruthie had left. Returning home from a business trip out of town, he literally went crazy upon finding her gone. He came to Rose's bawdy house several times, begging Ruthie to return home with him, berating and yelling at both Rose and Ruthie. Ruthie had planned her escape for weeks prior to his leaving on the trip, and shortly after he left she coerced one of the slaves into driving her into Millboro. Although it was really the only home she had ever known, it was still a tremendous relief to be away from him.

Shortly after arriving at the bawdy house, Ruthie had fallen desperately in love with Running Bear, one of the Indians in Robin's Nest. They trysted many times in the woods. Discovering herself pregnant, Ruthie retreated to Robin's Nest, where the Indians cared for her until the child, a little girl, was born.

Returning to the bawdy house, she left the child behind for the Indians to care for, visiting her from time to time.

Running Springs told me that Ruthie's little girl was named Cha-Ku-Ka, which means "of both kinds." When I later said this name to Jackie, she had an extreme reaction. "Chills went through my entire body, and my hair stood up. I literally felt my hair move." I told her it had been the name of Ruthie's baby.

A few years later, before her tragic shooting death in the whorehouse, Ruthie watched in tearful, stricken horror as her little girl, who was about three or four years old, along with the Indians of Robin's Nest, were forced to walk out of their mountaintop paradise for relocation on a reservation. The procession passed right by the bawdy house, and it broke Ruthie's heart. She cried and cried and tried to run after her little girl but was restrained by Rose and some of the girls. "You feel terrible, but what can you do? I know I will never see her again." The child was beautiful, had blue eyes like Ruthie's and dark hair like her father's. "I never saw him again, either. After the baby was born, we parted. The liaison led to disaster and was futile, so there was no reason to continue. But I loved him with all my heart. They watched, the Indians watched and kept him away. They didn't want a pregnant white girl living in their village."

Ruthie died soon after her little girl left, probably seven or eight months afterward. "It was tragic, a horrible, horrible life. Almost no happiness, ever!"

Running Bear stayed behind and took refuge in the woods, along with Little Eagle and several other braves. Before she died, Ruthie heard that he had joined another tribe, further west.

When asked about the smuggling that had gone on under the plantation house at Green Valley Farm, Ruthie exclaimed that it was a terrible worry to her. "But what could I do? I couldn't do anything about it. We all worried about getting caught; we would probably have been killed, just shot."

There were a lot of people in the area trying to help people get out of there all the time. They referred to the activity as simply "the Underground." She did not like to be around when it was being discussed; it made her nervous.

"Sometimes there were fires down there; they tried to keep warm. It was warmer down there than outside, but it's always damp. The number of men down there varies from time to time. They usually stay a week or ten days before someone comes to take them out."

Wrinkling her nose, she complained, "It's a terrible smell down there, smells like something dead. It is terrible—the soldiers, they urinate into buckets or wherever they feel like. It was not bad like that back before the war, when it was just slaves. There was not the stench; the slaves were pretty clean; some of the soldiers were sick, and they had been hiding before they got here, and they were real dirty. They were nice to me when I went down there, but they never bothered me. The old man never went down there, and I didn't tell him when I had gone down there either, because he was so jealous and possessive. I couldn't do anything; he would never let me go to any parties or social gatherings. I had no way to meet young men; he kept me on a very short leash. That is why I couldn't go to school; he had a tutor come in to teach me. I did not enjoy having sex with him. It almost killed him when I left to go into the bawdy house, but I couldn't stay there!"

She readily admitted that cannibalism was a fact of life during the war at the old house.

"They would feed them to the other guys. They brought them up from below and dressed them out; this was done in an old barn in back of the house that was formerly used to slaughter hogs. A couple of black men dressed the bodies, they burned and buried what was left over. They put the meat in a big pot and boiled it, usually with vegetables."

Elaborating on life in the whorehouse, she explained, "The girls in the bawdy house did things to avoid pregnancy. I had a tin thing, flat on one side; it looked like a half circle. It fit flat against the wall; it hung on a nail and I douched with it, put hot water in it and something . . . vinegar, that was it. I used it after each time and made the mixture very strong. I can see the hose, a tiny little red hose made out of some type of rubber; it had something on it so I could . . . cut it off, control the flow. I did not lie down to do this; I did it standing up and drained the water into a bucket. This was done in a small closet, off the room. I never got pregnant in the whorehouse, just with the Indian. He was nice, and I loved him very much!"

When Ruthie looked at pictures of the old plantation house, she gasped, "Oh, God, it's where I lived!" Getting very emotional, she pointed out the stone steps leading down from the pantry, above which has now been mortared over.

Studying a picture of the old whorehouse, she started to cry. "The house has a big woods out from it. I lived in that house, too; I was a prostitute there. There were lots of good times in those houses."

Later, in the conscious state, she declared that she just could not believe the pictures of the old plantation house.

"Does it still look like this now?" Jackie was amazed when she learned that the photos were taken only a few years ago. Studying the view from the rear of the house, she pointed out where the old slave quarters used to stand and was amazed to see the creek with almost no water in it. "When I lived there, it was very deep, very wide, and flowing, like a river."

Studying a photo of the old whorehouse, she asked, "Is there a big woods out from this, kind of a clearing, then a woods in back of that? It has always sat there all by itself, nothing around it. You come in off the road . . . this gives me goose bumps . . . it used to have a U-shaped drive up to the house. The room where I was killed was on the left hand side of this photo, in the back, above the bar.

Makes me nervous, kinda sad, nostalgic. Does anyone live in the house now?"

Jackie was, even fully conscious, seeing the house as Ruthie had many years ago. Obviously she was unable to grasp that the house is, today, barely standing.

Poor little Ruthie had almost no chance for a decent life. She left the plantation house that had been her home for most of her life partly to avoid being shot for treason, only to end up being accidentally shot and killed by a drunken patron at Rose's whorehouse.

While visiting Millboro in 1988 with Barbara Roberts, we set out to locate the old plantation house we had heard so much about. Inquiring of a woman in the nearby town of Warm Springs where we should start looking for a large, white plantation house in the area, that had in the past smuggled slaves, we heard, "Oh, that's the old Green Valley Farm. I have lived here all my life, and all my life I have heard stories about how they used to sneak the blacks out in the dead of night."

We found the place with no trouble at all, and the young man who was living there at the time allowed us to take pictures and graciously escorted us into the basement—a very small room. We could see where the old steps had come down from the kitchen above and observed that a brick wall had been erected in front of the arch-shaped door that led into the large room, which contained the tunnel leading out to the creek behind.

In the upper left corner of the wall, several bricks had fallen away, and I was able to see and touch the old wall behind the bricks. It was bilious green in color and made of concrete.

Pat Greene was born in Downey, California,
and has lived in Lake Elsinore for eleven years.
He is a professional sheet metal worker.
His secondary profession is that of musician and entertainer.
Until recently, he had never been to Virginia.
Pat's role in this story is that of John, the town marshal
in Civil War Millboro and Becky's husband.
Others had described much about John in Mission to Millboro,
but it wasn't until after its publication that we met Pat Greene
and were able to hear John's story from his own point of view.

CHAPTER 12

JOHN

IT WAS A FLASH OF RECOGNITION. Recognition, yet I had never lain eyes on the man in my life! This life, that is. The man was Pat Greene, and he had wandered into my peripheral vision as I stood in line at a fraternal lodge here in Lake Elsinore while waiting to be served a steak. Joe Nazarowski was cooking the steaks, and upon arriving at the head of the line, I asked Joe who the man in the black cowboy hat was.

Joe lived the character "Charley" in *Mission to Millboro*. "That's Pat Greene; he's an officer in the lodge," was Joe's answer.

Returning to my table, I suggested to Barbara Roberts (Liz in *Mission to Millboro*) that she look carefully at the man dressed in black. Gasping, she grabbed the edge of the table and, blanching, announced, "My God, that's John!" Liz was John's mother back in Civil War Millboro, Virginia.

A few weeks later I was a guest at the same lodge. Sitting at a table in the bar, I was suddenly confronted by Pat as he made his way through the tables towards the bandstand in an adjoining room. He was leaving to play drums with the band.

As he reached my table, and just before I recognized him, I was seized with a sensation that is really indescribable. It was weird, eerie, as though I was in the grip of some sort of electrical shock. My entire body was affected, and it lasted only the briefest of seconds. As soon as I consciously recognized him, it subsided. It was not because Pat is an attractive man. Other attractive men have passed by me, evoking little or no reaction. The sensation was strange and inexplicable, and I have never felt it before that time or since.

Shortly after my second exposure to him, I talked to Pat about the Millboro study and explained that it was highly likely he was involved. After *Mission to Millboro* was published, he agreed to take part in the research.

Pat's earliest feelings about John were in the Indian village, Robin's Nest. "Everyone works, in the village. Sometimes my mother takes me with her when she works, other times she leaves me with the older women who are in charge of the smaller kids." He was still breast feeding but old enough that he could go longer periods without food. Because he was cutting teeth, his favorite pastime was chewing on old corn cobs. By the age of fifteen months, he had been walking quite awhile and was called "Pony Boy" because of his unsteady gait. He staggered around like a drunk.

Sometimes during his fourth year, he and his mother moved into a house in Millboro. By that time he was being addressed as John. That same year he started school.

After *Mission to Millbor*o was published, there was a lot of speculation, verbally and in print, as to the authenticity and exist-ence of Indians near Millboro in the Civil War era, and even more about any area called Robin's Nest.

When this project first started, I contacted several members of the Ailstock family in various parts of the country, soliciting information about Millboro. Mrs. Cora Ailstock, of Waynesboro, Virginia, supplied me with news of the Indian village. Together with her husband, Tom, she had owned 200 acres of land on Tunnel Hill, in Millboro, so named because the railroad tunnel passed through it. To the rear of their property were located many Indian graves. Cora states that she heard her husband talk many times about his father, who was probably a Home Guardsman, "guarding for the Indians at the Big Spring, a few miles from Millboro, that the Big Spring was sometimes called the Robin's Nest."

John stated that some of the Indians on the hill were migratory; they knew it was a safe haven for "runners," Indians who hid to avoid being forced onto a reservation.

When John and Liz first left Robin's Nest and moved into town, they were miserable and homesick. They were ordered by the ruling tribal council to take up residence in town so that John, whose green eyes belied his predominantly Indian heritage, could be educated in the white man's school and hopefully return some day to teach the youth of the tribe.

All the familiar faces were gone, most of all Little Eagle, Liz's beloved Indian husband and John's father, who was forced to visit them only very late at night while the town slept. Consequently, when he was little, John saw almost nothing of his father. At about age seven, he started meeting Little Eagle in the woods on days when he was not in school. He would sit in the crotch of a tree behind his mother's house (that tree is still there today) and listen for Little Eagle's call, a cooing sound like that of a dove. Upon hearing the sound, he would scurry out of the tree and hasten to the special place where he met his father.

"It wasn't too far, but it seemed like I had to get wet, to cross a stream. I had a horse, a pinto I named Sunrise. That was because he was born at sunrise." Pat later said that in this present day life he had found a brown and white pinto and named it Sunrise, also.

John expressed concern as to where he kept the horse but suddenly realized that his father kept the horse for him and brought it with him when they met. He described a very soft saddle made of deer hide or something similar. It was soft enough to sleep on, on the ground, to use as a pillow. There was no need for a saddle horn, because Indians mounted and dismounted a horse by grabbing hold of the mane.

Little Eagle he described as tall, with dark eyes and hair, broad shoulders, dark skin, and wearing a light pullover shirt and long pants. His long hair fell down his back and was held in place by a cotton headband, such as tennis players wear.

It took Pat awhile to become conditioned to the hypnosis, and slowly, as John, he began to see the house he had shared with his mother. " I seem to see a side, outside, it's wood. Seems to be a green, dark green . . . wood siding. Below is some kind of a stone fire box, a fireplace. The wood seems to go down to the ground. I just see one side, trees all about. I keep thinking that I see a pan of some type, used for scooping water, bigger than a cup." His mother, Singing Bird or Liz (Barbara Roberts), who was hypnotized with him, said "It's a pan to wash from, but it's possible John could have drank out of it."

When we visited Millboro in 1988, we found an old wooden stand in a trash pile near Liz's old house. She said it had been hers, explaining later under hypnosis, "Mr. Phaelan made it for me; it was my wash stand. It set out there, and I could wash before I came into the house." Later, when conscious, she remarked, "The paths are still exactly where they were 100 years ago, tho' it's doubtful that anybody uses them now.

"One time, during the war, a Confederate soldier accidentally shot Little Eagle in the eye. Little Eagle startled the soldier while coming down a path; he always walked so quietly. It healed okay, but it was a couple of days before I saw him after that—he went to Mary's house (a neighbor), and she tended him. She wanted to get me, but he wouldn't let her get me."

Liz wound up her monologue with, "My clothesline was missing. It was between the house and the chicken coop, made of metal wire. I tripped and fell into it the day I died. They buried me in town somewhere, but after awhile, Little Eagle and another Indian moved my body to the Indian burial ground."

When John started school, Liz did not take him, despite the fact that he was only four years old. Someone named Stella used to pick him up in a wagon—Stella was probably the teacher. Liz had a lump in her throat the first day he left her, but she knew he had to go, because the council had decreed that he must learn.

John's description of the Guy Fawkes day party seemed pretty tame compared to how Becky and others had described it (in *Mission to Millboro*). Finally we figured out he was viewing it as a fairly young boy, when the celebration was in its infancy. By the time Becky attended, it had become a full blown affair. As he described it, he was sitting, unobserved on the periphery, watching the event. Everyone was dressed up, almost formal.

We had asked him about the booze, and laughingly he replied that he was too young to drink, but from the expression on his face we knew he had. "The booze is served in little Mason jars, and everyone has one. I know where they hide it and could easily snitch some if I wanted to."

His strongest impression of the party was everyone dressed in their church clothes, the men in black bow ties and hats, sitting around long tables eating endless mounds of corn on the cob. There was no awareness of music and dancing, but maybe he was gone when that occurred. There had been two large bonfires; over one they hung the figure of a man. He clearly saw the church but said that early on there was no barn; that had come later, when the whole town turned out for the festivities. At the later, livelier parties, the small children were put up in the hay loft of the barn to sleep.

Frequently, during his weekend trips with his father, they would go out in the hills and visit "the red-haired boy" (White Bear). He always took a bag of food and clothing with him for the boy. Sometimes the bag would encumber him as he climbed the tree to await his father's call. He flashed on White Bear as a red-haired boy, orange-haired actually, who wore bib-overall type clothes and resembled the Howdy Doody character today. White Bear blew a flute, not well, which Little Eagle had made for him out of a reed-like plant of some type.

Little Eagle taught John how to shoot with a bow and arrow, which was better for hunting, because it was silent. Later, he was allowed to shoot a rifle, but he had to earn that right.

From earliest infancy, John had been imbued with the necessity of keeping very quiet about his heritage. It was dunned into him constantly by his mother, and later, as he spent more time with his father, the reasons were explained to him in detail.

Until we met and talked to John, we never really stopped to consider what it would be like for a man, three-quarters Indian, to be raised as a white man in those days. How divided were his loyalties; how threatened would he feel by possible exposure? The average American today has little or no conception of what it was like to be an Indian in the early and mid-1800s. Consider first that the status of the Negro was that of sub-human and its intellect primitive and inferior at best. A lot of white people had themselves convinced that blacks were born solely to serve whites. On the status ladder, the Indian rated far below the Negro and was truly considered by many whites as no better than an animal, and was treated accordingly. Marriage between whites and blacks or whites and Indians was unthinkable and, furthermore, illegal. Blacks and Indians were denied education of any kind, and any slave owners caught teaching their blacks to read and write would be punished under the laws of the land.

Had the truth ever surfaced that Liz was one-half Indian and John's real father 100 percent Indian, disaster would have rained down upon them. By law, John would have been expelled from school, and both would have been ostracized and run out of town, either back up to Robin's Nest or, more likely, banished to a reservation. There were two significant factors that buffered them from a potentially hostile society. Liz had the prestigious Ailstock name from an earlier marriage, and both of them appeared Caucasian, thanks to their light skin and piercing green eyes, both of which were heritage from Liz's Irish father.

It is generally agreed among the people in this study that Pat Greene more closely resembles his Millboro counterpart John than anyone else involved in this story. His personality today is that of John's—affable and very likable, intense, dedicated, close-mouthed, excellent sense of humor, extremely stubborn, and thoroughly involved in any cause he supports. His appearance, right down to the burning green eyes, is almost identical to John's.

When *Mission to Millboro* was first published, a party was held to pass out books to the participants and to introduce those who were strangers to one another. Because Pat Greene was involved at that time, he was invited to attend. Diana Lovegren, who regresses to Elizabeth, John and Becky's youngest daughter, also attended. Elizabeth adored her daddy and rhapsodized endlessly about his good looks and charm. One time, when she was very small, he had given her one of his old hats as a birthday present, and she prattled on endlessly about how she cherished the hat and wore it everywhere. John's trademark, according to Elizabeth, was his ubiquitous black hat.

Taking Diana's hand at the party, I led her up to Pat and introduced them. Diana stood as though riveted to the ground, her eyes transfixed on Pat's green eyes. Finally, tearing her gaze away, she glanced at me and asked in a firm tone, "Where's his black hat?"

The question arises constantly why the people who lived 135 years ago in Millboro, Virginia, are again together in Lake Elsinore today. There is no ready answer to that question. The one common denominator is the fact that both towns are the site of artesian, sulphur springs. Elsinore, for many years, had a heavy spa traffic. Wealthy people from all around the world plus many Hollywood luminaries came frequently to take the baths.

This traffic has tapered almost to a standstill, thanks in part to heavy flooding several years ago, which caused the city to disconnect most of the sulphur water pipes. The town of Millboro appears to have ignored any commercial exploitation of the sulphur springs under the town, but they are there nevertheless.

Earlier in the regressions, Becky had talked a great deal about the fun she and John had had in the sulphur water hot pools, admitting that at least one baby had been conceived there. John discussed the pools, too, stating there were two sites in the area. One place had one pool, and the other, three. When he was a youngster, he and his friends played in the three-pool area. They used to swing on ropes above the pools, then let go and drop in. They played in the pools, but the actual bathing, with soap, was done at home.

On our recent trip to Millboro, Maureen, Smokey, and I spent a lot of time in Millboro Springs searching for the site of the sulphur pool. Maureen kept leading us to the edge of the road, insisting the springs were nearby. Finally the owner of the local general store informed us, "The springs were there until about the 1930s, then they were filled in, and the highway was built over them!" Such is the price of progress!

The white boarding house, John said, was pretty much in the center of town and was the only building there that was painted. All the rest were raw wood.

Sometime during the early part of the war, a bank vault was brought into town. Charlie and Becky had laughed over this episode, describing how it had smashed the wagon they put it on and how, finally, in desperation, the team of horses, which was secured to the vault by leather straps, had dragged it through town to the bank. John elaborated on this story.

"It was made of steel, about the size of a septic tank. It came in on a flatbed, and they slid it down on pipes onto the wagon, which broke to splinters under the weight. Then they put the vault onto rollers, possibly the axles of the wagon, and slid it to the bank. They had built a new bank to hold the vault, and no one could figure out why they would order a vault after the bank was built. That's like trying to put on your underwear after you have your pants on." The bank at that time was a small wooden structure near the general store. According to John, it was necessary to tear out part of the building to insert the vault.

Katy, the town prostitute, for whom Katy's tunnel was named, was a friend of John's, despite the fact that she was much older. In the beginning, she operated out of the boarding house, but when Honey took it over, that ended that! This would have been around the time the tunnels were being built and was probably the reason Katy began operations in the tube.

"I see a short, blonde-haired woman, who was really a very nice girl. She looks a lot like Doris Day."

Laughing uncontrollably, John described how he became Millboro's lawman.

"The Sheriff's Department wanted volunteers. I was the last one to be asked. The question we were all asked was, why did I think I was qualified for the job? Everybody else just said that they thought that they could do the job, and I said that I could beat the shit out of them both and still do the job. He (the sheriff) had had someone else before, but he had screwed up. I wasn't being mean when I said I could beat the shit out of both of them and do a good job; I meant it. I laughed about that for years. The story got around, because the Sheriff told it to everyone. My mother knew I was going to say something like that before I ever said it." He carried his badge always and sometimes a gun. The badge said *Marshal,* or possibly *County Marshal.*

"People come to me for advice, and I keep peace and quiet. Everybody trusts me, and I can talk to them." His badge he wore on his shirt, under his jacket, and he displayed it when he felt it necessary.

John was about twenty years old when he became the town's lawman; he married Becky not long afterward. The town was not rowdy in those days, despite the existence of three bars. After their marriage, he and Becky moved into the little white frame house. Slowly they set about turning it into a productive farm. There was a "barn-raising" one afternoon; most of the town came, and after the barn was up they did a little drinking . . . homemade whiskey and punch. The remark about the homemade whiskey reminded us about the stills in the area, but he refused to discuss them.

"I know everybody around here," was all he would say, and the message conveyed was that he looked the other way.

They had horses, cows, chickens, a dog, and rabbits—no children yet at the time of the barn-raising, but he thought one was on the way. Sometime after Elizabeth, the fourth child, was born, John told Becky that he was predominantly Indian. Until that time he had led her to believe that he and Liz were of French descent, an easy lie to sell with their coloring. He had never planned to tell her; did not think it was necessary. Unfortunately, his mother decided that Becky should be let in on this deep, dark secret and informed John that if he did not soon tell her, that she, Liz, would. Becky's reaction was something neither of them had expected. At first she refused to believe him. Nothing was ever the same after that; she looked at him differently, and it seriously affected their marriage.

"She did not love me the same after that." He had real pain in his voice. "I can't know what she thought—I think she thought I had tricked her."

Knowledge of this terrible secret completely undermined the structure of Becky's life. Until then, she had felt safe and secure in her marriage and her position in society. Suddenly it was all threatened. John was a half-breed or, as contemptuously labeled then, a "breed." The only thing lower than an Indian, on the status scale of the time was a despised "breed." John was a "breed," as were all four of Becky's oldest children. Another stigma would have been that the children were illegitimate, as there was no legal marriage between whites and Indians then. Should this awful truth ever out, none of them would have been tolerated in the town.

Until hit with this news, the marriage had been rock solid. A devastated Becky struck back the only way she knew how. With the help of her friend Constance, she started a line of affairs with other men that continued until and eventually caused her death. Becky denies she was racist, that her only reason for upset was that he did not trust her enough to tell her up front. However, her later revelations and display of attitude regarding the lot of the Negro race strongly belie this. When asked if she would have married him knowing of his Indian blood, she shook her head vehemently and spat out NO.

Looking at the year 1861, he said, "There's things going on to indicate a problem. Lots of people escaping, going to the North." He was referring to the Underground Railroad smuggling operation, helping slaves escape to freedom. "Mostly black people are coming through now (as opposed to later on when wounded and escaped Union soldiers used the UGRR to escape to the North). They are afraid that if the South is not part of the United States, they will be worse off. Also, from them we can find out that the South is preparing for this problem, they are training military groups all over. They are civilians, but they are getting ready, practicing to fight. They are more serious about it than the North—the North does not believe them; the North does not take it seriously."

When asked about the supplies piling up all over town, he responded, "The South is doing a lot of buying, storing supplies. Supplies came into Millboro after the South became more familiar with Lincoln; when they thought he might win, they started ratholing stuff. They said that if he was elected president, they would secede."

That he become involved in Union intelligence was suggested to him by his father. The majority of Indians strongly supported the

North. They had seen firsthand how the blacks were treated by slave owners in the South and knew that if the South were to win, their lot would only worsen. They did not trust the North to any great extent, but they trusted the South even less. The Indians were John's couriers, delivering messages wherever they were destined.

Rose came into town and opened the bawdy house soon after the war started. John claims that he never really knew for certain that she was sent to spy, but that it made sense. She may have been a counterbalance to him.

"If the Union hears something from her, and then they hear the same information from an Indian, they will know it's true."

He did, however, glean a lot of information from her. Drunken Confederate officers tended to become very talkative in the whorehouse. As to leaving much written information in the boarding house for Union couriers, he denied that. "It doesn't sound right, leaving information under the mattress in a room in the boarding house. I don't think I would do that. Nothing written."

He continued, "The Indians dealt with both sides, Union and Confederacy, and were pretty much ignored by both sides. They went almost any place they wanted to, rode horses from place to place, and were never suspect."

One of the primary questions raised in *Mission to Millboro* was, knowing that Millboro was crammed to the rafters with Confederate supplies, why did the Yanks never attack the town?

"The Union Government knew all about those supplies backed up all over that town. They didn't attack it because of the UGRR. That operation was a two-way door; it swung both ways. We took Negroes and Union soldiers and spies out and brought supplies and other spies in . . . and we did it all right under the nose of the Confederacy!"

He was a lot more in control of that town than we had ever realized. He kept the Union army out, ostensibly to keep the door open to the UGRR, but basically he was doing it to protect "those people up there on the hill. Nothing will happen to them as long as the situation remains status quo. My sympathies were with the Union, but I had the confidence of the Confederacy and the townspeople. That town was so busy trying to get those supplies in and out, and the Confederacy was so busy, they didn't have time to do anything but fight the war. The Union would leave Indians alone, even protect them, even take care of them, if they needed it. It was basically a Union town, but the Confederacy didn't know it. The majority were Union, but the few who were Confederates were very vocal."

That was part of John's deal with the Union, that the Indians were to be taken care of, and the Indians knew who was protecting them. At the time, the Union was fighting for individual freedom, and the Indians were lulled by this. Later, John did not even try to hide his bitterness at the Union for running his people out of Robin's Nest a few years after the war ended.

In 1860, there were approximately four million slaves in the Southern states, one-third of the South's population. Exactly how long the Underground Railroad flourished is problematical, but about 200 years would be a safe guess. Slavery abounded in this country back in the 1600s, and most Christian religions, some more so than others, were vehemently and vocally opposed, pronouncing the bondage of man by man an abomination in the eyes of the Lord! It was primarily the religious groups, especially the Quakers, who precipitated and organized the UGRR.

John admitted freely that he knew what was happening in town as regards the UGRR, and that "I would protect the people who were doing it. I might take an active part in it from time to time, but only when I have to."

He insisted that people were not hauled about in coffins, as we had been told earlier, but that they were hidden in gun boxes. Guns back then were very long.

"You could take the boxes out, unload them, knock them down, bring them back, and use them again."

The town was unique, in that it was one of the few places where one could smuggle Union soldiers and spies in and out with impunity. The Confederates had no idea any of this was going on, according to John, and if the Union had gone in there and said, "This is our town," then it would have shut down the thoroughfare that the UGRR provided.

"From the 1700s until the Civil War, that UGRR had been going. The people there who did it were going to continue to do it, and they were very quiet about it."

While looking at the picture of the Green Valley Farm, he immediately made a reference to the basement, but cautioned that we must not talk about it. He stated that the old, white-haired man ("Colonel Lewis") was much respected in the community, and that very few knew that he smuggled slaves. He could see another house on the far edge of Millboro that hid slaves.

"Sometimes they came in on the train, then jumped off before it got into town and ran up a hill to a place of safety."

The discussion of the UGRR ended with this statement: "There is a tunnel from the railroad tracks that leads into the basement of the house in town that hides slaves."

At first this idea was tacitly discarded as being improbable and unrealistic. However, later testimony of others in the study tends to lend credibility to the idea.

John resisted discussing Becky and her death, but did admit that he had been aware of her love affair with Charley and that it had probably crossed his mind that blond baby Peter was not his. The baby most certainly did not look Indian. Later, in the conscious state, he said that his pride had been wounded; it would just hurt to bring it up, so better to ignore it. "There were more important things going on back then; a lot of things seemed more important."

Becky was killed, he thought, because she knew something of what he was doing and talked. As far as Jake was concerned, "There was some money involved." Regarding the shooting and hanging of Jake, he said only that a law man would not have done anything like that. "Did I ever admit doing it? Why would I say I had done it?"

On a trip to Millboro later, I took Pat Greene (John) to the site of Becky's grave. He immediately pointed to the area where she is reported to be buried and said that he and the children had outlined her grave with rocks, about fist-sized. This matches a statement that Elizabeth also had volunteered to me at an earlier time.

CHAPTER 13

JOHN OBSERVES

THE ROOMS AND TUNNELS UNDERGROUND had been built long before he was born, John confided. "They were there, and it was just a strange coincidence that I even found out about them. I found out from the Indians."

He thought that maybe the Indians had helped build the rooms, and more than likely they had made the mixture, now green, that lines the walls. His mother, Liz, had claimed awhile back that the Indians had made the bricks that line Katy's tunnel.

"They chopped up a certain type of grass that grows in the area and put it in the concrete mixture. The grass reinforces the concrete, makes it tough as steel," was her comment.

John never actually went down into any of the rooms. "I couldn't go down there, not with my job."

He was not certain how many "safe houses" there were in Millboro. The one in the picture, Grandma's house, he was sure of, and there was another one, about a mile out of town above the railroad tracks. It was a white frame house that sat on a hill over the tracks. He had seen the colored people jump off the moving train and hightail it up the hill towards that white house.

At an earlier time, it was John who had announced decidedly that there was a tunnel from the railroad tracks up to the room under Grandma's house. He, like Sally, was vague about where the tunnel opening was near the tracks. He felt there was a smaller shed or house somewhere, which was the entrance and exit to the tunnel that led to the hidden room. Possibly he was thinking of the shed at the rear of the property, which may have been a late-night exit for refugees, but which would have been terribly exposed during the daytime as an entrance. It seems impossible that fugitives could have gone into that shed undetected.

It has been suggested that the opening of the tunnel was in the crotch of the bridge crossing the railroad about a quarter of a mile from Grandma's house. Time will tell.

The Presbyterian Church above Grandma's house was definitely involved in the smuggling of slaves, and the activity was well supported by the congregation.

John did not think there was a hidden room in the church, but that there was definitely a tunnel leading from the rooms in town into the basement of the church, and when they thought it was safe, they sometimes brought the people there and kept them.

"It was a logical place to take them out, actually, rather than leaving at night. A lot of people go to church; nobody counts how many goes in or how many comes out. That's the time they came out, when church was letting out; they mixed in with the crowd. It was done quickly, and most of the people in the crowd were not even aware it was happening."

When the subject of the old bottles (presumably liquor) found in the hidden room came up, John strongly opposed the idea that there were ever Confederate soldiers under the house.

"They may have hidden there after Grandma was gone and no one was using those rooms; they may have stumbled on it amongst themselves, but nobody would have allowed anybody they knew was a Confederate to find any of those tunnels, not while the war was still on. It was too easy to have an infiltrator find out about the operation and expose it. I would have thought that the Confederate deserters would have just gone up North, completely out of the way. I would not have thought that they would have exposed any of the rooms to the Confederates, not intentionally. You still had Yank soldiers, still had slaves; it's not a good mix. Not after all the years they spent building those rooms to free those slaves."

He continued, "I get the feeling that some people think that trainloads of slaves were coming in and going through the tunnels and rooms. There was a very small amount of people at any one given time, because you just didn't have a lot of people who could make it, or who even knew where to go. You have a few coming in, but you didn't have like thirty or forty people all at one time; they would just come in bit by bit. It was a stopover, a safe place, while they continued North. They were hunted down, shot; it was not easy for them, because of their color, to hide. The people did not stay real long, usually only a week or so. It was as safe as they could be, but at best it was dangerous to be there—a lot of Confederate soldiers around. It was a place to stop, get a breather. The Indians helped a lot, getting them further north after they left Millboro. The Indians were pretty safe at that time; the Confederates were concentrating on the war and getting those supplies out. The Indians were instrumental in getting the people out after they left the church. The whites would smuggle them a ways out of town, probably in a wagon, meet the Indians at a designated place, and the Indians would lead them, mostly on horseback, through safe trails to the next stop," (which was very likely the plantation house in Green Valley, due north of Millboro).

John did not identify any other houses in town that he thought had rooms; he just kept remarking about the white house about a mile before town. He described it as a big, white, pretty house with white pillars, a kind of southern plantation type.

Gazing at a picture of the hidden room, he remarked on the pink pipe in the picture. "I think that was a communication, into the other room, but mostly upstairs. They could hear things and they could talk."

Later, when conscious, he said there definitely was a talking pipe from the room up to the house.

"It came in at the stone fireplace. Under the mantel there was a tiny gap; it appeared as though the caulking had fallen out, and you talked and listened there. If you didn't know exactly where it was, you would never spot it."

Normally, the hypnosis sessions with John (Pat Greene) were a depressing experience, because there was very little happiness in John's life. When we started this session, he was given a piece of soap that Maureen had recently made. She remembered exactly how Becky had made it, so she decided to make a batch now. He recognized it immediately; said it was soap either his mother or Becky had made. Then he was handed the remains of the large granite bowl found at the site where Becky and John's house had stood. His face beamed; we had never seen him look this happy.

"I ate soup and stew out of it. I like this; there's something about it, this particular bowl. Beef and rabbit, lots of vegetables."

He said he thought it was grey with white speckles, which is correct.

John's final statement was, "It's hard to piece all the little things together. I guess what I felt was right in my heart was my overriding dedication to the Indian cause and, looking back, I should not have married and had children, but of course we would not have known that when I was young!"

CHAPTER 14

SAMUEL

When Samuel's story appeared in *Mission to Millboro,* it raised some questions. Samuel (Ralph "Smokey" Williamson) claimed to be from Roanoke but, as several readers pointed out to me, Roanoke as a city did not exist then. The town that is now Roanoke was then called Big Lick. After looking at an old (1860) map of Virginia and talking to Samuel some more, we were able to solve the mystery and will explain it all a little later.

During our first interrogation of Samuel, he was breathless and excited, explaining that he was being chased. He had been stealing guns and was caught. It was Confederate soldiers who were chasing him as he drove a wagon loaded with about one hundred guns. At that time he abandoned the wagon, ran up a hill and into some woods, and got away.

He explained that his actions in Millboro had been predicated by his transportation into town. If he rode in on horseback, he interviewed a few Confederates for his newspaper, perhaps saw Becky, and left. If, however, he brought a wagon, he spent more time, loading his wagon with Confederate supplies, mostly guns and sometimes blankets (which were in great demand). He took the guns from the supplies that were stacked all over town, had to take them one at a time, hiding them under his coat. They came in boxes, twelve to a box, but one was all he could manage at a time. They were very long rifles and, according to Samuel, were really beau-

*Ralph "Smokey" Williamson was born in Michigan.
Currently he is employed as a firefighter.
He has lived in the Elsinore area for twenty-five
years, and prior to this study he had not been to
Virginia. He has visited Millboro once
after the story was published.
His role in the story is that of Samuel,
a newspaperman who was also a Union spy,
as recounted in* Mission to Millboro.

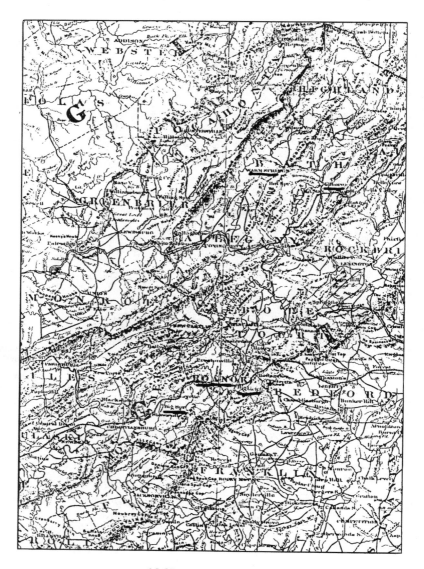

1865 map of Virginia.
Underlined: Warm Springs, Millboro, Roanoke County,
Big Lick, and Big Springs.
Colton's Topographical Map, courtesy of Sterling Memorial
Library, Yale University, New Haven, Connecticut

tiful. He thought they had been made in Belgium; the South had no
facilities for making guns.

There were several people in town helping him filch supplies,
including John. They would steal a gun whenever possible and
stash them in the shed until Samuel came to take them out. "It was
extremely easy to take that stuff. They would be standing guard at
the front, and we would steal it from the back. It was in piles, very
disorganized."

Samuel would take the guns and anything else that had been
stolen from the Confederates to another distribution point, where
the stuff would be smuggled on up North. He also went to Millboro
to give and get information to pass on . . . the number of troops
assembled, troop movements, and the different supplies that were
coming in. Usually the top intelligence people could learn a lot from
the types and quantity of supplies that were arriving in town.

Samuel made no money from the transfer of guns. Most of his
profit from the war was from selling medicines, which he garnered
from the Millboro supply dump, and booze, which he purchased
cheaply from local stills and sold at an outrageous profit to Confederate troops.

Samuel volunteered that he had to use a different road leaving
town than he used coming into town. There were regular check
points where they searched wagons leaving town on the traveled
roads. Strangely enough, according to Samuel, Union forces did
not jump those wagons very often, because the roads were pretty
well guarded. There were no decent places for an ambush of any
kind. The road was pretty straight, with no places to hide, and the
places that were hideable was where they had their check points,
extremely well fortified.

He could not be gone too long on these forays, because he
would get too far behind. While in Millboro, he interviewed a few
soldiers; he had his favorites. They were stupid and unknowingly
gave him information he needed, especially after he plied them with
whiskey. But, according to Samuel, a lot of the stuff he printed he
made up. This gave him more time to concentrate on stealing guns.

During the course of the Civil War, Samuel had interviewed
many military men. When he was shown a photograph of General

William Tecumseh Sherman, he laughed long and hard. "He was a crusty old general who did not like reporters. He never smiled, because he had wooden teeth that clacked when he talked. It was a very disconcerting noise, which embarrassed him—a very abrupt person who had no time for reporters, would not allow them on his base. He reminded me a lot of Napoleon, a small man complex."

Samuel stated that he had been desperately in love with Becky. "I loved her more than I did my wife. My wife was a sickly, prudish person who would not undress in front of me. I have no idea what her body looked like. On the other hand, I had no problem knowing about Becky's body. She had her clothes off in the blink of an eye. I always thought I was just a toy for her, and it hurt me."

Constance was a big factor in breaking up their romance. It seems Constance had an eye for Samuel and was jealous of Becky. She knew Samuel was married and threatened to expose the affair to his wife. "It had nothing to do with the gun running. She was going to write to my wife. Stay away from Becky, or she would tell my wife, which would have blown my cover, probably would have caused my death. My wife was a very vindictive person, and she likely would have turned me in to the Confederacy to get back at me. Becky never knew this, never knew why I broke it off. She was always in my heart, and it was very painful."

He carried a large torch for Becky the rest of his life. "I would see her in town, and it would tear my heart out." After her death, he had considered doing a story about her for his newspaper, but he was afraid that anything he wrote would expose his feelings for her.

When discussing his home town, on several occasions he said, "Big, it's Big something."

Later he stated that the town was called Big Springs, and Becky piped up that if it was Big Springs, he would live near her. She was referring to the area of Robin's Nest, which was also called the Big Spring.

Pinning Samuel down, we learned that he had been born in the Kansas territory and moved to Virginia when he was little, and that his name was Samuel Phaelan, or possibly Pelter. They moved to

Roanoke, which he claimed was at that time a township or maybe a county. He lived in an area called Big Springs, about three or four miles from Big Lick. He had one sibling, an older brother. When the boys were older, their parents moved up to Warm Springs, near Millboro. Samuel and his brother Felix (a name he hated) remained in Big Springs. They had some land, and Samuel was then a jack of all trades, did some carpentry work, and sort of "piddled about." When his parents moved north, they had left some money with the boys, so they were under no pressure to work.

After awhile, Samuel married a girl through a correspondence match-making agency, a girl from Chicago. When his parents died a few years later, Samuel, his wife, and brother Felix moved to Bath County. At first they all lived in the parents' plantation house, but soon Felix was smitten by a young lady named Carolyn in Millboro, and he moved there, married, acquired a lot of land, and raised horses.

Samuel took over the responsibilities of running the plantation, as his brother wanted no part of it. There was a large house, a lot of land, and several slaves who lived there. Samuel said they were pretty free to come and go as they chose, but they did work the land and were his property and had to be seen to.

His life was serene until the onset of the war. When he was approached by his brother and John to spy for the North, he looked about for a cover. He was able to read and write well and enjoyed doing both.

"Did not know anything about the printing business when I got into it, but it was a good cover. I bought a print shop and had it shipped down and set up. It proved to be a real good cover, and I enjoyed it, as I was extremely nosy, anyway."

The paper, called the *Pen and Quill,* he mailed out of Millboro. It would attract less attention being sent from Millboro, he thought. "It was slipshod; it went out when I had information. It was really more of a bulletin, a newsletter type of thing."

There was a man named Chad in Roanoke, one of the spy ring that the newspaper was basically geared towards, as the thing was loaded with coded messages. There were subscribers, mostly Union spies, and a lot of copies made their way to Washington, D.C., hand carried, passed from person to person through what they called the grapevine.

The Phaelans were a prominent family in the area, both Samuel in Warm Springs and Felix in Millboro. This had a lot to do with why he feared exposure of his romance with Becky. His brother was his only living relative and had no inkling of the romance with Becky, and Samuel lived in terror that his brother would learn of it. Despite all the factors against him, Samuel reiterated that he loved Becky deeply and had she fought breaking it off he would not have done it. He was a lot older than Becky, and he called her "Free Flight," like a small bird that never settled in one spot.

He had seen her from afar and admired her for a long time before meeting her. Their meeting in the woods one day was not the accident that we had been led to believe. He had arranged to meet Becky, knew where she would be walking, and just happened to be there. He salved his conscience with the knowledge of John's affair with Rose and knew that Becky would discover John and Rose's liaison before too long. When he broke it off, he knew Becky was pregnant, but he had never worried about getting her pregnant. "When you made love to Becky, you didn't think about anything but making love!"

While in New Haven, Connecticut, awhile back, I was able to obtain a copy of an 1865 map of Virginia from Yale University. On it, one sees Roanoke marked as a county, with the small town of Big Lick and the tiny town of Big Springs a few miles to the west. Big Lick has since been redesignated as the city of Roanoke, and Big Springs is no longer. Samuel had been absolutely right about the names of these areas.

When Samuel was asked if he was aware of the Underground activity in Millboro, his answer was really surprising. Despite the fact that he was an active saboteur and a member of the Union spy ring, he was a plantation owner who kept slaves, and it is logical to assume that he knew nothing of the movement to free slaves.

"I stayed away from them (the rooms), because I didn't want to be associated with them."

Then he proceeded to tell us that Grandma's house above the general store had two rooms underground, and that there was a smaller house off to the west somewhere. It was a rust-colored, one-story house. At night they signaled their contacts by putting lanterns in the windows, either one or two lanterns depending upon whether there were slaves or Union soldiers, or both, who needed to be moved out. Above Grandma's house, up the hill and off to the right, was the large, two-story stone house that others had described. He had been down in that room, the largest in the Millboro area, one time. Admitting that it was a stupid thing to do, he explained that there was someone down there being smuggled out, to whom he had to talk. In the little house out of town, there was a trap door built into the floor near a fireplace. Samuel ended by insisting that the bottles found in the small room under Grandma's house had been put there by escaping Union soldiers or possibly after the Civil war ended. In concert with everyone else in this study, he insisted there would never be Confederate soldiers allowed into any of those hidden rooms, deserters or not.

"The Union soldiers would have killed them. Nobody trusted anybody then!"

Rock Rest, as the old Bratton house is called today,
is one of the oldest houses in Bath County.
A Civil War skirmish was fought in the yard,
resulting in bullets being fired into the house.

Bratton's Bridge, now located a few miles out of Millboro,
on property owned by the Persinger family.

The Cauthorn farm today.
It stands directly over the railroad tracks.

of Two Thousand Five HundreD Dollars($2500) in hand paid, the receipt whereof is hereby
acknowledged. The said parties of the first part doth sell and convey with general warrantie
and in fee simple of title unto the said parties of the second part, a certain tract or parcel
of land lying in Bath County Virginia about two miles east of Millboro and lying on the east
side of the C&O. R. R. adjoining the lands of J. M. Bratton and bounded as follows:-
Beginnig at an iron stake on the East side of said R. R. on said J. M. Bratton,s line by a
fence S 38-½ E 92 poles with said Bratton,s line and fence to a black oak with the top
broken off(old line marked) five black pines marked for this survey. N 63-½ E 92 poles to
a stake black oak. White Oak, hickory and pine pointers N 37-½ W 91 poles to a pile of stone
on the East side of said C &O R.R. S 66 W 12 poles up the east side of said R. R. to astakeS
S 63-½ W 84 poles to the beginning containing fifty two acres being apart of 647 acres.
The parties of the forst part further grant unto the parties of the second part, the Right
of Way over aroad now leading from said 52 acre tract crossing the R. R. crossing Bratton,s
Bridge to the public road at apoint nearing the grave yard, but eserve the right to hang
necessary gates over said road. Witness our signatures and seals the day and date above
written.

```
-------Witness at signing---            __M. Eleanor Bratton ( Sel )__
Geo. M. Taggart, asto Margaret M. and   ___Margaret Moore Bratton(Seal )__
Martha E. Bratton, Wm. H. Frick.        _____Matha Elizabeth Bratton(Seal)_____
```

On the twentyseventh day of September 1913 before me A Notary Public for the Commonwealth
of Pennsylvania, residing in the City of Philadelphia, personally appearedMary Eleanor Brato
and acknowledged the foregoing indenture to bo her act aHd deed and desired the same might b

Excerpt from old deed (1913) that names Bratton's Bridge.

CHAPTER 15

BRATTON'S BRIDGE

WHILE EATING CHILI DOGS at the Millboro General Store, Smokey (Samuel) looked up from the Bath County map and announced, "We have got to find Bratton's Bridge." The bridge was plainly marked on the map, and when I asked why we had to find it, he replied, "John and I pulled a bunch of trapped Yanks out from under that bridge. It was a very tense situation."

So started the search for Bratton's Bridge. It shows very clearly on the map, near the junction of the main highway leaving Millboro for Goshen and a smaller road coming down from the north. Smokey was adamant that there were more than one set of railroad tracks near Bratton's Bridge. We inquired at the Millboro General Store and heard, "Oh, that's down near Bratton's Cemetery." Bratton's Cemetery is right off the main highway, and we had passed it several times, so we returned to that location. Inquiring at several homes in the area, we struck out completely. We crossed over one very old bridge a couple of times, en route to a lovely house high on a hill. Unfortunately the residents were away, and Smokey said no, that could not be it, because there was only the one set of tracks nearby.

Finally we parked the car and walked for several miles along the tracks. Nothing. Next morning Smokey decided we had been walking in the wrong direction, so we returned to the site and walked for miles in the opposite direction. We found nothing but a railroad switch box, which indicated that there was or may have been a railroad spur in the area at one time. In desperation, we drove towards Goshen and stopped at a small store along the way.

Smokey was laughing as he returned to the car. "You're never going to believe this. We have driven over Bratton's Bridge several times. It was the old bridge we carefully crossed that leads up to the large house on the hill."

It seems that prior to the Civil War, the railroad had installed a logging spur onto the Bratton property to haul out timber. After WW II, the lumber operation was shut down and the railroad spur removed. That accounted for the switch box we had found the previous day. That also explained why Samuel thought there should be more railroad tracks than there are today.

Documents sent to me by Mr. Harry Jolly of North Carolina, whose mother was a Bratton, relate to a battle fought on the Bratton farm in 1864. The old Bratton house, named Rock Rest, was built in 1806 by Major James Bratton, a hero of the American Revolution. William, the son of James, was a member of the Lewis and Clark Expedition. Several bullets were shot into Rock Rest during the Civil War skirmish.

That evening, Smokey, hypnotized into the role of Samuel, related the dramatic saga of Bratton's Bridge. Somehow John, very late in the war, received word that there were several Yanks trapped in a cave under Bratton's Bridge. He hurriedly recruited Samuel and the young Negro boy, Coffee. "We figured, what the hell, Coffee was black and could probably sneak in there if we couldn't."

He continued, "It was Coffee's idea to tie blankets around our feet so we wouldn't make noise in the cinder bed. He said we should walk like Indians, but those blankets almost became our undoing when we got to the creek. It was late August, just after the rains, and the creek was full. Locating the blankets was no problem; it's amazing what you will find on clotheslines."

They waited until the dead of night to launch this dangerous expedition. Pulling charcoal out of the fireplace, they darkened their hands and faces with it and put some in a canvas bag to take with them. Earlier they had tried lamp black but discovered it washed right off in the water.

The three of them walked stealthily down the tracks. It was easier walking on the tracks, but when they got within sight of the bridge, they knew they had to get into the water. "Man, that water was cold! We could hear the Johnnies; they were laughing and carrying on, smoking cigarettes. They were on top of the bridge and had no idea what was going on beneath them. Coffee was leading the way; the water was running real deep as we got closer to the bridge and . . . he drowned. We didn't know he couldn't swim. We figured they could all swim. He was a brave little bugger, though; he gave it his best try; didn't splash around or make any noise. Just disappeared. Never even found his body. Maybe the blankets pulled him down. It was over all our heads; I got a couple of mouthfuls, and it was nasty tasting, bad!"

Coffee was, Samuel said, about eleven or twelve at the time of this expedition. This did not jibe with what Baby Peter had said previously—that he used to play with a little Negro boy named Coffee. At first he said Cocoa, but we corrected him and asked if the youngster's name may have been Coffee, since Coffee's name had been mentioned by others. In light of the drowning incident, Peter's little friend must have been the real Coffee's little brother, as Peter's friendship with the black youngster took place a few years after the war ended.

In the creek, John and Samuel continued on, trying to tread water, keep their heads up, and not make any splashing sounds. They could hear the Confederates overhead, noisily talking and laughing, unaware of why they were guarding that stupid little piece of land. Probably the Confederacy was aware that there were Union stragglers in the area; perhaps they had even chased them there, but most certainly they were unaware that they were standing right over their heads.

It was a fairly large cave; there were eleven men in it. They had been trapped in the cave for almost a week, with no food except what they could trap out of the creek, mostly rats and animals that had drowned. They did not dare move about much for fear of being heard. Except for the noise made by the Rebs on the bridge, it was so still and quiet on the night of the rescue that one barely took a deep breath.

These men were cut off from the main body of troops. They were lost, wandering around, when they decided to follow the railroad tracks. Samuel and John thought they were trying to get into Millboro, hoping to tie in with the Underground Railroad, when they were discovered.

I asked Samuel, "How did you greet them when you joined them?" He answered, "Very quietly. We sneaked into the cave, and they could tell by our appearance that we were not the enemy. We had no guns, because they would have made noise and would have been useless due to the water. We had to take all their buttons and wrap them with cloth so they wouldn't be seen. It was in the darkest part of the night, about two or three in the morning. The Confederates were all asleep by then. They were tired, had not eaten anything, and had not been relieved, so they just went to sleep.

"The men were pretty weak and beat up; they were just thankful to sit down, and they thought we were crazy! We had a real hard time convincing them what we were going to do. No, they didn't want to get into that ice cold water. We gave them a choice; they could stay behind if they wanted to. They talked to each other and they all came out. Followed us like little lambs."

For light they had something called "lucifers." They were matches, much longer and larger than any we have today, and they burned for a long time.

The rescuers had brought charcoal in a canvas bag and made the men blacken their faces and hands. They had also brought some hardtack, which was the first food any had eaten for several days. It had gotten a little soggy in the water but they ate it anyway. Then they led them slowly, in a chain, out of the cave and into the water. John and Samuel both situated themselves at the head of the column, then if something went wrong and they were fired upon, if they went in different directions they most likely would not both get killed. The men were treading water as best they could. A couple of the younger men could not swim too well, but their buddies helped them. None of the men were lost; they got them all out. The caravan stayed in the creek until the leaders deemed it safe, then they took them up onto the tracks. The rescued men were tired, sick, and some could barely walk. The biggest problem, according to Samuel, was trying to keep them quiet. After their terrible ordeal, the men were running on nerves, adrenalin flowing, and so excited they could scarcely contain themselves.

Samuel and John led the men towards town and left the tracks right at the big house up on the hill, the one that sheltered the slaves. There they waited for the go-ahead signal, a lighting system. "If there was one light, it was okay to go in; two lights meant stay away. There was one light that night. We already had it set up; they knew we were coming."

When asked how long those boys had been in the cave, Samuel replied, "I have no idea; that wasn't our job."

The family that owned the house Samuel thought was named Ridgeway, Paul Ridgeway. Later he said that perhaps Ridgeway did not own the house but was instrumental in getting them into it that night.

I asked Samuel what else he would like to tell about the magnificent rescue that he and John pulled off that night.

He answered, "Well, I was glad it was over with, and I had a cold for awhile that was hard to explain. I stayed in town, in the shack. We got some everclear (homemade moonshine liquor) and it kinda cooked the cold a little.

"The whole thing did not take too long, we were well over with it by daylight."

Still hypnotized, Samuel was brought up to the present time, and he stated that the bridge we had found was a part of the original structure. A little bit of the cave remains, under the side of the bridge, although it is pretty well covered by the railroad ties that reinforce the bridge. A lot of the cave has been filled in, due to high water at times. Samuel noted that there was no reason for us to go looking for it, as it has been mostly obliterated.

Thereafter, in the conscious state, Smokey reiterated that it was really black on the night of the rescue; they had a hard time finding the tracks and the creek. The single light burning in the window of the rescue house was a really welcome sight to the soaking wet, cold, badly frightened men. "The house was owned by a man named Cauthorn, whose mom was nuttier than a fruitcake. I think that everybody thought she had some sort of disease, and they didn't want to get it, so they all just left her alone. No, she didn't do it on purpose; she was nutty. Acted like she had been whopped up along side the head once too often. She would sit and talk to herself, play with beams of light; she would talk to the beams of light. They kept her in the top of the house—put her up there so she could play with the sunlight . . . and the dust. She used to drive them buggy downstairs, because she would stamp her feet to raise the dust so she could play with it. She was nuts!"

Samuel always wore a greatcoat. It was his uniform. The night of the rescue, John would not let him wear it. "He said if I wore the coat into the creek, it would get cleaned and people would know I had been up to something. We had a hard time with the blankets over our feet; they were over our boots, and we had no idea the creek was that deep."

In trying to figure out how the men in the tunnel got the word out regarding their plight, we decided that someone must have escaped, or possibly, because the Cauthorn family, who owned the house at that time and still do, were members of good standing in the Millboro Presbyterian Church, maybe a Cauthorn youngster discovered the men and told their parents, who in turn got word to John.

The story obviously made the rounds of those "in the know," because when Honey was shown a picture of the bridge later, she recognized it immediately. "I have been over that bridge. There's a lovely home above. That bridge is beautiful . . . there was . . . a lot of soldiers hid under there; we heard about them being led out of there." Asked about Coffee, she said, "He disappeared after that. He went up into the hills; that's the story that went around town. It was a mystery—he just disappeared." She became very upset when she heard what had really happened to him.

Later Samuel stated, "We took them to the big house, the Cauthorn house. We didn't dare go near the house, but we pointed them in the right direction and sent them up the hill."

About Townley Cauthorn, the man who built the white house over the railroad tracks, Samuel said, "He was not a local boy, came in with the railroad. Opened a store in competition to the general store. His stuff was a little higher class, flowered glass lanterns, fancy things. Cauthorn built the house after he married a local girl, a Bratton. One could see the slave quarters behind the house. Behind the slave quarters was the underground room. There's a small shack over it; looks like a privy. Having the room out among the slave quarters made sense. Who's going to know who's who? Nobody counted. We had a scare there for awhile, because the Confederacy tried taxing them, the slaves, which would mean you had to have the same number all the time. The slave owners raised so much cain they finally backed off."

When conscious, Smokey claimed that today the room is partly paved or graveled over, like under a driveway.

John and Samuel used to make homemade bombs, according to Smokey. They shaped wet flour and gunpowder into a ball about the size of a fist and dried it for a few days in the sun. Then they would wander, socially, into a Confederate camp and, unobserved, drop one into a fire over which the soldiers were cooking their meals. After awhile the thing would blow up with a loud noise, scattering food, clothing, and anything else nearby. It was totally unnerving to the men, and they never did associate it with the two visitors, as they were long gone when the thing blew.

When Smokey first brought up the subject of Bratton's Bridge, several local Millboro people denied any such thing existed. Harry Jolly said he was well aware of Bratton's cemetery, but otherwise had never heard of Bratton's bridge. I responded that it had to be the one over Mill creek in front of his old family home.

A few months later I received a copy of an old deed dated August 20, 1913, which sells part of the land that three Bratton sisters owned. The deed states that the property begins "at an iron stake and goes to a black oak with the top broken off, to a white oak, to a pile of stones. The buyers are granted right of way over a road leading from the 52-acre tract that crosses the railroad track and *Bratton's Bridge,* to the public road near the grave yard."

One has to wonder if the pile of stones is still there.

Millie Sproule, born in Alabama in 1928,
now works as an office manager in a family business.
She is the mother of two daughters, lives in Lake Elsinore,
and has never been to Virginia.
Her role is that of Honey,
matronly owner of the town boarding house
in Civil War Millboro.

CHAPTER 16

HONEY

HONEY (MILLIE SPROULE) was one of the primary characters in Mission to Millboro. She was the matron who ran the boarding house in town and was pretty much beloved by all.

When she looked at a photo of the Green Valley Farm, her comment was, "That's where we went to the dance."

John had taken them out to the dance. There were a lot of people in the wagon—Liz, John's mother and Honey's dear friend, was there, and "even Hoppy was there. (Hoppy Harper was an unkempt, part-time fur trader, who did odd jobs for Honey's husband, Thomas.) He rode in the back. He stayed outside—he was so dirty, they would not have let him in. He took care of the wagon, stayed with the horses."

They had had a wonderful time at the party. "We had food, ham, and cakes and grits, punch. We did not take it; it was already there—they fed us. It was a big party. They had a round dance; we did not do the Virginia reel. We danced in the round; we just all held hands and round danced, but mostly it was with couples."

John had convinced both Honey and Liz to go out to the party; he had known that Philip would be there. As related in *Mission to Millboro,* Honey had known Philip before she married Thomas and always said she should have married Philip instead of Thomas. (Later, after Thomas was killed in a card game and the war ended, she did.)

Honey knew about what was going on down in the basement of the old plantation house, "We weren't supposed to know. There's people down there, blacks. They stay down there for awhile, then they take them to the North. Some of them come in wagons, and some of them walked, they walked for a long ways. There's another way out . . . a long tunnel. Way in the back there's a stream, a lot of trees. There's a chain of houses that help these people. When they started smuggling Union soldiers out of the basement, then is when it became so dangerous. Until then it was not so dangerous."

When she went out to the party at the old house, "There was just the older white-haired man and someone else (perhaps Elizabeth) who was helping out, not the man's wife. He is old, white-haired, dresses real well; looks like he's got money."

Honey claimed that she had no direct dealings with the UGRR, but she knew a lot about it and knew that John was somehow involved in it. "There's a lot of them that go through there; it's been going on for a long time, since the 1700s. They come in wagons. Sometimes they come in on the train—they jump off before the train comes into town." Very seriously, she added, "Oh yes, they jump off a mile or so out of town, they don't dare come into town. They come in mostly at night."

When she was asked about the house in town where they had been helping these people for a long time, she said, under her breath, "Mr. Cullins. There's two houses, one on the left and one on the right. The one across the tracks is Mr. Cullins' house. His wife is named Bertha, Bertie. It is a big house, two stories, tall, white."

When asked how they get into the hidden room, Honey said, "It's like a storm cellar thing. You lift up a door, go down these steps into a tunnel. That is where the tunnel is, in the little shed that's used for storage. There's plows and all kinds of junk in there."

We asked how far the shed was from the house and heard, "From here to yonder." Honey was never one to be pinned down.

Honey said that Bertie had a little girl she was raising (which would be Sally), and that the child had died from a fever after having been sick for a long time.

When she looked at the picture of old Millboro, she immediately pointed to the same house that Sally had designated as Grandma's house. Honey said that she could not see the house today, but that the shed was there, and there were trees all around it.

"People who have lived in that house probably don't know about the tunnel and room. In the house one picked up a plank to go down; there's a rug over it and a table on the rug. In the shed there's junk, sacks of stuff, over the trap door."

Others had spoken of the ill-fated demise of "Grandma's" smuggling activities, which is described later (in chapter 19), but Honey was vague about what happened to "Grandma" (Bertha).

"She just disappeared, dropped out of sight."

CHAPTER 17

WILL

AFTER ONE OF THE TELEVISION SHOWS featuring the Millboro story, my telephone rang one day, and it was Diane Bock, an Elsinore matron. She explained that her daughter, Lyne, was very excited by the story and felt that she fit into it somewhere. We set up an appointment for me to regress Lyne.

As with my daughter Evie, Lyne regressed back into the life of a young man during the Civil War era. These two and Joann Kelley (Soaring Eagle) are the only subjects in this work who regressed back into members of the opposite sex. This man's name was Will, and he was the complete antithesis of Lyne today. Will was very tall, about 6'4", thin, lanky, with auburn hair and light eyes. Today Lyne is short and ample, with blond hair. Both, however, give indications of having an extremely high I.Q.

When the regressions began, Will was happy and loquacious. As the sessions continued, however, he became more and more moody and morose. The Civil War period was one of extreme sacrifice, hardship, and irreparable heartbreak, especially for those dedicated to the Confederate cause. Will was one of these. In addition to the sadness generated by the war, he was possessed by a consummate anger that eventually took over the hypnosis sessions. We were able to get the greatest part of Will's story but, towards the end, despite any suggestions I gave to the contrary, it became difficult for Lyne. She is glad the story has been told, and

Lyne Bock was born in Santa Ana, California.
Currently she is a student and
has lived in Lake Elsinore since 1978.
She has never been to Virginia, and her role in the story
is that of Will, head of the Confederate spy ring
in western Virginia.

> Special - Secty of War ...
> Valley Head Alabama
> 19 June 1861.
>
> His Excellency Jefferson Davis.
> President of The Confederate
> States of America -----
> Dear Sir:
> I was Cadet in
> the Military Accademy at West Point from June
> 1859 till about the 1st of January 1861, at which
> time learning that Alabama had a majority in
> convention for immediate secession I resigned
> my position.   On my return home I received
> a Commission of 2nd Leautenant from Gov A.B.
> Moore, was ordered to report myself for duty
>
> looked.   I am in the 22nd year of my
> age: Have made the military art my study
> during the last four years. I understand In-
> -fantry Tactics and have some knowledge of
> fortification and field artillery. I now
> tender you my services, and am ready to
> occupy whatever position in the Regular army
> you may decit to be assigned me, hoping
> and believing that I can render some aide in
> the defence of the Independence of our beloved
> South.   I am Sir most respectfully
> Your obt Servant.
> Wm O. Winston Jr

*Beginning and end of a two-page letter
that Will wrote to Jefferson Davis.*

she cherishes the memory of Will, but all things considered, she is glad it is over and that she is able to put it in the past.

Will's mother was a Northerner, possibly from Vermont. His father, however, was a regular army officer from the deep South.

He had an older brother named Steven and a younger sister, Cynthia. Like all military families, they moved a lot, from base to base. He said his mother was not very happy with the military way of life, as it meant that for the most part they had to live in outposts far from civilization, away from the culture and refinements she enjoyed. She was very careful not to let Will's father know that she was unhappy.

At the age of seven, Will said they were "in the woods now, waiting for the military to come and get us. We are traveling with other officers' families, traveling in wagons—about fifteen large wagons, mostly loaded with pianos and other household stuff. I don't know my dad's name; I call him Captain. Want to say the fort is named Bragg, but that's not it. My father is an army man, but the station is a cavalry post. Lots of horses, and he does a lot of riding. The tutor teaches all the kids together in the mess hall, roughly ten or twelve kids in all. Some of them are really little."

Progressing ahead to age fourteen, they were again moving. All were very nervous, and he thought it was because they might be in Indian territory. "They haven't built the fort yet; we are waiting for it to be built. My dad is off supervising the work, and we are afraid of the Indians."

By the time he was fifteen, they were further away from the proposed fort. It had become too dangerous where they were and the Indians so hostile that they had fled to a cabin in a remote, wooded area. He thought it was Wisconsin. Snow covered the ground, and it was very cold. They were waiting out there in the woods for the fort to be secured. Some sort of problem existed with the French people; he was unclear what the problem was. They were sequestered in a hunter's cabin, and the place was crowded,as there were a lot of people with him. Will and the men spent a lot of time hunting, to feed the group. His father was away, off at the fort with his men.

In early spring of his fifteenth year, Will's mother and his sister were murdered in an Indian massacre. Will, his older brother, and some of the other men were on an overnight hunting trip. A few men were left to guard the women, but they were overpowered. It was his opinion that the Indians had been drunk when they did it. Possibly they had come in and drunk with the few men who had been left as guards; then, with enough liquor in them, they went crazy.

Because she was part Indian, his mother had always gone out of her way to treat Indians with kindness and respect, offering them food and other amenities.

When the bodies were discovered, they had been dead about twenty-four hours, "We decided to stay and wait for them to come back. We knew they would return, because they hadn't taken anything. They would come back to take what they could off the dead bodies. There were about thirty men in our party, and we were very well armed. We couldn't bury the dead, because we didn't want them to know we were back. About a week later, they showed up; we sent out scouts to watch for them. We were hidden, some in the cabin and some outside in a half-moon, crescent-shaped formation. They didn't expect us to be there, and they had no idea how many of us there were. There were about fifty of them. We ambushed and shot them; I was shooting from inside the cabin. Some of the men wanted to hang them, but it wouldn't have been right. Besides, there was not enough rope.

They weren't all Indians. Some were French. We killed the Indians and captured the French, made the French dig the holes to bury our people and the Indians. It was early spring, and the snow was just beginning to melt. Indians were dressed like the French men, cloth shirts, regular trousers; some wore buckskin. We did not bury the French, just left them to rot!

We asked Will how they differentiated between the French and the Indians, whether they looked alike. He answered, "No, they don't. They had different colored skin, and the French had mustaches; they like to wear the bushy ones. Indians don't have mustaches, except the half-breeds. We killed them, too; they didn't deserve to live."

Will stated that the scene of the massacre was horrible. The bodies had been scalped and mutilated beyond recognition.

The site of all this horror was somewhere in the proximity of Canada, and the Indians and French were much further south than they were supposed to be. The father had been gone for months. "He was more worried about the fort. We would have been safer in the fort than where he left us!"

When she was killed, Will's mother had been young and, according to him, very beautiful. She was tall, graceful, and had auburn hair like his. After the massacre, Will, his brother, and their father left the wilds and returned to civilization. His father retired from the military, and a few years later, at age nineteen, Will entered West Point. Will said his father was about sixty when he left for West Point, but records I located later indicate he was closer to seventy.

July, 1859 found him standing in front of a big gate. He had been traveling, had a suitcase with him, and was shivering, despite the fact that he was wearing a coat. Obviously, he was nervous, as were some of the other young men milling about, waiting for the gate to open.

A few months later he was standing on the parade ground, looking up at one of the buildings. It was night and it was cold. There was a girl in that building, and Will was hoping she would look out the window and notice him. She was the daughter of one of the officers stationed at West Point. Will had met her soon after his arrival and was very taken with her, mentioned her frequently during the sessions, and even tried to locate her after the war, to no avail.

Later we found him wearing a cadet uniform and studying in the base library. "It was important to my father to get me into West Point, and it's important that I do well here. My father is a West Point graduate." This last nugget of information was instrumental in helping me identify both Will and his father when I later visited West Point.

When shown a picture of Charles Patterson, a look of instant recognition crossed his face and he stated that "Charley sounds right," as regards his name. "He was older than I was, graduated sooner."

The next hypnosis session brought Lyne together with Joe Nazarowski (Charley). Will opened the conversation by explaining that his mother had been from the North and his father was a devout Southerner, but that he had been raised in the backwoods and that North and South had not been important where he was raised. Evidently he had stumbled into the political tug-of-war between North and South that was raging at West Point about that time.

Charley stated that Will was a lower classman who was a tall, lanky guy with brownish auburn hair. He had a problem because he was so tall; he stood out like a flagpole in formation. He was about six foot three or four inches; you put that six or eight inch plume hat on him, and he stuck out like a pole, tallest in his class."

Will admitted that he got a big kick out of George Custer. "He was a total ass; that's what I liked about him. He was so funny. Everybody knew he got through by cheating. He was a conceited, arrogant ass." The incident related by Charley in *Mission to Millboro* about Custer tripping the cadets with the wire stretched across the steps had occurred prior to Will entering West Point. When he heard what had happened, and that the other cadets retaliated by filling his shoes with molasses, Will howled with laughter. Charley added, "He had to wear them them all day with molasses in them, and he didn't trip anybody anymore." Will's attitude towards Custer was that he was a constant source of amusement, but Charley was not so tolerant. "He should never have graduated. He got into West Point through political pull."

Will was a couple of classes behind Charley. "Basically, how Will and I got involved was that I chewed his butt! He was so tall, it was easy to pick on him. He had some problems, but he wouldn't come to the upperclassmen, tho'; he would do everything on his own. Proud and stubborn."

They were assigned cannon duty together, and Will was placed in one of Charley's squads. After they cleaned the cannon, he would put the powder in and tamp it, put the charge in and wad it down.

A short time after the session with the two men, I again visited the archives at West Point, armed only with the knowledge that Will was about two years behind Charley and that his father was from the South and a West Point graduate. I started searching the records.

Checking the class of 1863, I was unable to locate anyone named Will or William who had defected to the Confederacy or whose father had been a Point man. Finally, almost by accident, I located a book listing West Point attendees and there, big as life, I read,

William O. Winston, graduated 1812, commissioned 1st Lt.
William O Winston, Jr. resigned Dec., 31, 1860.

Both men entered West Point from Valley Head, Alabama. Then it hit me—of course Will had left the Academy. Alabama was one of the first states to secede, and Will had entered from Alabama. Because he failed to graduate, there was no picture of him available.

Will had stated that he hit the books a lot, determined to get good grades. His record shows that he was fifth in a class of forty-one students. About the only other record of young Will Winston is his name in the demerit book—page after page of demerits—strange for one so devoted to his grades.

In my next session with Will, the lead-off statement was, "Let's talk about demerits." The response to this was a loud giggle. I continued, "You are fifth in the class academically, but you have all these demerits. Why don't you show up for breakfast and lunch?" Continuing to laugh, he exuded a "don't give a damn attitude" and said, "They just have it in for me, the instructors. I don't eat much; food's not important to me. I just want to study all the time." Was it really worth three or four demerits just to miss lunch? "Yeah, I don't care. (hedging) I usually don't talk much to people. Seems it's my father I am mad at; it's his fault my mother died."

Changing the subject, I inquired about the political tenor of the time and heard, "Oh, yeah, they push you around because your father's from the South. You push back; then you get into trouble. I don't care if they kick me out; the Union's gonna split anyway. I am so mad." Will claimed that he did not approve of slavery but believed strongly in state's rights.

Charley stated that from the time of his class on, all cadets were warned, "Don't graduate and then quit and go into the Confederacy; that's considered cowardice in the face of the enemy. There was more of it in later classes, as the war progressed. The lower classes would do anything they had to, to get a commission. If you had two years at the Point, they would bring you in as a sergeant. They wanted you to have full training."

In the conscious state, Joe explained why Charley was on Will's butt all the time. "He was a big, tall cadet, and I knew he leaned towards the Southern cause. West Point is a training ground for officers, and I figured he would end up in the Confederacy. It was not a matter of liking or disliking; I wanted him to graduate with honors. I would double-check his homework.

Lyne stated that she reacted to Joe as Charley the minute he walked into the room. Laughing, she said, "The first time I saw him, I felt compelled to jump to attention and brace, and my stomach knotted up. That's why I declined when you offered me a soft drink."

CHAPTER 18

WAR'S END

UPON RETURNING FROM West Point, I immediately requested information from the archives in Washington, D.C., concerning the William O. Winstons, Junior and Senior. There is no information whatsoever on Senior, but I received a large packet on Junior.

Among the papers were: a document from the Adjutant's office at West Point confirming his resignation from the Academy; a letter from the Executive Department (of the Confederacy probably), confirming that Winston had applied for a commission in the Confederate Army; a letter dated 19 June, 1861, from William O. Winston, Jr. to the President of the Confederacy, Jefferson Davis; and a letter dated October 29,1861, from William O. Winston in Valley Head, Alabama, to J.P. Benjamin, Secretary of War of the Confederacy. In this letter he explains that since January he had been drilling volunteers for the Southern reserves, that he had applied immediately upon leaving West Point for a commission in the regular army, and that obviously that letter had been overlooked. Evidently there was some mix-up regarding his age, because he wrote another letter to Benjamin, assuring him that he was twenty-two years old. Several other letters from local politicians and high-ranking friends of his father strongly recommend that he be accepted by the Confederate Army.

There were several copies of pay vouchers—then suddenly I came across a very chilling document. William O. Winston was accepted as an officer cadet in the Confederate Army on December

Class of *1863*.

Name *Winston, William O., jr*
(Surname)   (Given name or names)

Appointed from *6 Ala.*
(District and State)

Admitted *1* *July* *1859*
(Day)   (Month)   (Year)

Age at date of admission *19* *9*
(Years)   (Months)

Legal residence *Valley Head*
(Town)

DeKalb *Ala.*
(County)   (State)

Name of parent or guardian.
Wm. O. Winston

Residence of parent or guardian.
Valley Head *Ala.*
(Town)   (State)
(Street and number)

Order of general merit: — *5th Class — 41*

(Fourth Class Year)   (Third Class Year)

(Second Class Year)   (First Class Year)

Remarks *Res. Dec. 31, 1860*

Wm O. Winston Sr.
grad U. P. 1812
1st Lt.

A. O. U. S. M. A., Jan., 1915.

*Information
form of
Will Winston
from West Point*

2, 1861. He died April 11, 1862, at Chapman's Fort, South Carolina of . . . *measles!* This information devastated me, since I was so certain that Will Winston was the man who's life story Lyne had been telling me while under hypnosis. Reeling from shock and disappointment, I mulled this entire situation over in my mind for a few days, and then, like a bolt from the blue, I was inspired, remembering the very first regression I had held with Lyne, when I had heard, "I am a man, in the South Virginia, wearing a grey uniform. *I am a spy,* a scout; we are looking for something."

Shades of Charles Patterson! Scheduling another appointment with Lyne, I regressed her to the life of Will and suggested it was the second week of April, 1862 and he was at Chapman's Fort, South Carolina, and how did he feel? "Very badly. I have a bad cold, my throat hurts, and I have pains in my chest, along with a high fever. For the past few days I have been in the hospital with pneumonia."

No, there were no spots on his body. No, he definitely did not have measles. He started to laugh and admitted that the "measles" routine had been his idea. He had been terribly frustrated during his cadet training (this is reflected in the letters he wrote). Finally, the Confederacy decided his talents were being wasted drilling cadets, and they accepted him into the regular army. It was his idea that he become a spy, and the Confederacy readily agreed. "They were going to train me, but they discovered I was very proficient. There were not too many Confederates who had been raised by a mother from Vermont. I had no trace of a Southern accent."

When he became ill, they saw their chance to spirit him away. He suggested they label his pneumonia as measles so they could quarantine him and isolate him against visitors' prying eyes. As soon as he was well enough, he placed a dead body in his cot. "There were lots of dead people in there. It was night; I dressed in civilian clothes and simply walked out of the hospital." Someone was waiting for him outside the hospital in a carriage, and they took him to a campsite to meet with some high-ranking general. He adopted his mother's maiden name, which he thought was Anderson, and from that point on he was under cover.

Still not absolutely convinced I was talking to Will Winston, I took him back in time to June 19,1861 and told him that he had written a letter to a fairly important man. Who was that man?

"I write a lot of letters, am really angry! It isn't right what they are doing; I am just mad! They have me doing kitchen duty, digging holes, training men, drilling men. It is not important work. I want to get out of here and fight. I can see myself writing the letter—want to say I wrote to Davis, Jefferson Davis."

This was another time when chills traveled up and down my spine. I was sitting there with a copy of the letter that a frustrated Will had written to Jefferson Davis, in my hand!

Will's undercover assignment was not as concise and clear-cut as Patterson's was. He traveled continually, sometimes with a squad of men, sometimes alone. On several occasions he mentioned meeting with President Lincoln. He claims he went to see the President after he went undercover for the Confederacy. "I wanted him to stop the war. I saw him a lot; we met out behind the White House. His guards were there, but not too close. They looked the other way, because he told them to. Mr. Hobbs, that is what they called me." Will had several meetings with Lincoln, a few times prior to joining the Confederacy and a couple of times afterward. He suggested that he may have been related to Lincoln or Lincoln's wife; that might explain how he got in to see him so easily.

Will worked with a great many people. He went into Union territory frequently and took information into Richmond on a regular basis. Not just a spy, he became head of the entire spy ring in the western Virginia area. "I had to meet with people and go to them, as they could not leave, especially the ones up North."

His work towards the end of the war had something to do with all the supplies stockpiled in Millboro. Frequently, he and his men would oversee the moving of those supplies.

The first time he went into Millboro, he spotted Patterson and said it was a real shock, because he had thought Charley was dead. The two men did not acknowledge each other, as each was under cover. Will said, "I was shocked when I recognized him, both because I thought he was dead, but mostly the way he looked. Fat, scruffy, he looked awful. No doubt it was part of his cover; (laughing) it was a hell of a cover."

Towards the end of the war, Will spent most of his time in the Millboro area.

There was a strong and angry reaction from Will when the Underground Railroad was mentioned. "It makes everybody mad—they have no right to do that! We have spies that tell us lots of houses are doing it; we have to find out which ones and stop it!"

They frightened the people in the town, told them they were traitors if they refused to talk or report which houses in town were smuggling slaves and Union soldiers. Finally, a terrified woman pointed out a large house atop a hill in town. Will and some of his men went into the house. It was a big, two-story house with lots of rooms, and the woman who owned it denied there was a hidden room. He located "a yellow and white door; it looked like part of the wall. I had to duck, so it must have been under some stairs. It looked suspicious; that's why I kicked it in. It was a door, and it swung in, splintered when I kicked it, knocked it off the hinges. There was a drop into the room; I kinda jumped into it. It was about the size of a small bedroom, about eight by ten feet. There was a door that led outside; that's how he left. I was looking for some one, the spy. His name was John."

This last revelation was a surprise. Will explained that he had orders to arrest John and had been tracking him for days. "I would catch him out of the corner of my eye, and before I could do anything about it, he was gone. He moved like a *damn Indian.*"

He reacted strongly when I showed him a picture of Pat Greene. "My God, it's him!! He was head of the Union spy ring in that area, and that's why we were after him. It was kinda like a chess game, one spymaster after another. He was pretty smart, but not as smart as he thought he was. We knew he would be in that one particular room, but of course he was gone when I broke in. People had been there; you could smell them. There were blankets, plates—some-one left in a hurry."

In a way, Will explained, he really did not want to catch John. It was like a game, and "we were both playing the same game."

When Lyne came out of the trance, she marked an O on a big house in my picture of old Millboro, to indicate the house Will had raided. It, today, is realtor Larry Fresh's house.

General Lee had given orders that Confederate troops not waste time trying to locate the Underground stations, as by this time the war was going so badly for the South that they could not spare men to conduct such a search.

Will had another surprise for me. He declared that Mr. Warren, the man who ran the general store, was really an avowed Confederate, that all the ardent conversation in favor of the Union was just a cover up. "We could go into his store, tell him we were General Lee's boys, and he'd give us anything in the place. We never had to pay for anything. We did not get paid too often, never really had any money, ever."

In the early spring of 1865, the war was winding down. Will and his men were "in the mud—we hate the mud." They were sick, miserable, it was cold, wet, and they had no food. He went into "Marlboro" to get supplies. His contact was probably Charley. "He looks older, his hair is long; he is very miserable, disappointed in life. The war did not turn out as he had planned."

Will did not return to Valley Head, Alabama, after the war. He just let his father and the rest of the family think he was dead. He went up to stay awhile with his mother's family in New England and eventually went to California.

He continued to feel nothing but bitterness and hatred for his father, blaming him for the death of his mother and sister and for all of life's failures. "I don't think he was really my father. He didn't care about the girl, either, just the oldest son." This was a son from a previous marriage; his first wife had died. Will's mother had been pregnant with him when she married Will, Senior. They met at a social gathering in a large city in the Northeast. He needed a wife in order to fit into his military career properly, and she needed a husband for obvious reasons. Will was named Junior so the world would think he was Will Senior's son. Will Senior was very bitter, cold, and hard. "He wasn't surly; he didn't rage or anything, but he was just quiet, cold, and uncommunicative." Will's real father was very much in love with his mother, but he had died before they could marry.

There was almost no joy in poor Will's life. All he had really wanted was to pursue a music career. "I wanted to work on my music; I played the clavichord." He had spent a lot of time mastering the instrument; his mother spent hours teaching him. His closest friend and confidante had been his mother, and when she was so horribly killed, the spirit died in Will.

CHAPTER 19

CHAOS

"I THINK GRANDMA GOT . . . CAUGHT! Somebody in uniforms. Confederate soldiers. They shot her!"

This happened about two months after Sally died, but she was still able to see it clearly. Perhaps it was inevitable that eventually one or more of those involved in the UGRR activities—"Grandma," Mary Alice and her husband Henry Wilson (the undertaker), Allie Morgan's family, Col. and Mrs. Lewis of Green Valley Farm, and possible others—be discovered.

"It was dusk when Grandma was shot. A couple of men came running into the house; they were a mess, all ragged and filthy."

At first she said they were Confederate soldiers who came into the house, but that was pretty much discounted, so we decided they were escaping Union soldiers. She admitted that their clothing, such as it was, was so ragged and filthy that it would be impossible to tell what they had once represented. Whoever it was, they panicked and ran into Grandma's front door.

"They came into the kitchen, and Grandma hid them in the woodshed, back of the house off the kitchen. Two more men came in through the front door, just ran in and surprised her. They were Confederates in beige uniforms. (Toward the end of the war the South could no longer get the grey dye from England that they had been using.) They wore big hats and guns. There was a lot of yelling; Grandma was throwing pots and pans and screaming for them to get out, amidst a lot of scuffling and yelling. The first men got away during the fracas, then one of the Confederates took out his gun and shot Grandma, and she died almost immediately.

After they executed Grandma, the soldiers spent a couple of hours searching the house but did not find anything. Obviously they were looking for the hidden rooms.

Grandma was left where she fell, in the kitchen. She was wearing a long dress, white with tiny flowers. The neighbors heard all the racket and later came in and found her. They had a quiet ceremony and buried her somewhere secret, then put out the word that she had gone to live with her daughter in another state. Grandma's husband was dead. She had owned the house, cooked and baked a lot, a great deal of which she sold. This covered the fact that she had a lot of food on hand to feed the people below.

Sally claims that there were no escapees in the room down below Grandma's house when she was shot. As a matter of fact, they had just left. Sally had never seen either of the two men who ran into Grandma's house and executed her. One was "real tall, thin—he has a real mean face with a square chin. His face is real wrinkled. The other one is kinda big and heavy."

The incident of Grandma's shooting sparked several weeks of utter panic, chaos, and dread in Millboro. It was Mary Alice, the undertaker's wife, who first described the chaos that ruled the town in early January, 1865, in those first few weeks after Grandma's death. "Something's happening. Everybody's running around and talking. I don't talk too much; it's like if I don't get involved, then I won't get hurt. I don't want my husband to go away, but he's talking about leaving. There's something frightening the people of this town. It's scary! People are getting killed; they are pulling people out of their houses and accusing them of things and shooting and hanging them. It is a gang of people—some in uniforms and some not. They are all yelling and screaming and accusing people of stuff. They are shooting guns into the air and into the ground, holding nooses and ropes, and threatening people with their lives. They are questioning people about, trying to locate a group of people who were operating in that town. They were looking for . . . they didn't know what . . . there was something going on in that town and they were looking for it. Later there were renegade mobs, ex-soldiers dressed partly in uniform. I can see the leader of one; he has a kerchief around his neck, wears a duster. The kerchief is red and white, tied in a way so he could pull it up over his face. I think they killed people—not any of the townspeople, but people on the road. The refugees were the ones they preyed on. These interlopers were really evil. There was no law and order in town towards the end of the war; everybody hid in their houses and was afraid. It was almost worse than wondering if the town was going to be invaded. I did not worry about the Yanks coming into town; what I did expect was that all of us could get caught. If they had caught the husbands, they would probably pick up the wives, and there was no telling what would happen with the children.

At a later time, Sally and Allie discussed it together. "It was utter turmoil, chaos. We're so tired—children crying, people running and screaming by the railroad station. Soldiers and men who were supposed to be family friends; they did terrible things to the people. They had long guns with knives on the end; they poked and prodded people with the knives and tried to get them to tell where the Negroes were hidden. They wanted the black people and the people who were saving the black people, and they threatened anyone in town who they thought knew anything and who would talk. They even threatened the children, and some of the people had to talk. They found only one or two of the rooms and a tunnel that came out on a hillside, in a clearing." That was Sally speaking, and then Allie added that there were a whole lot of men, maybe twenty or thirty, all dressed differently, some in uniforms, some not. "People that you knew and thought were friends, they claimed that somebody in town was making money and they wanted to find out who, perhaps to try to get some of the money for themselves." Very angry, these men were trying to find the Underground Railroad and find out how much money the people were making.

It has been said that in an attempt to discredit the UGRR, the Confederacy started rumors to the effect that people running the UGRR were charging escapees exorbitant sums of money to take them to freedom and were becoming millionaires. Some Southerners, too ill-advised to realize that no escaping slave would have access to any large amount of money, naively believed this fabrication.

Later, we asked Honey how the Confederates found out about the hidden rooms. Her answer was that she really did not know but that you cannot keep something like that a secret. When I answered that the secret had been kept for almost one hundred years, she replied, "Yeah, but not that good. People knew. They weren't running soldiers, and there wasn't a war on."

Honey hid in her boarding house during the weeks of terror, and the ruffians did not bother her. Charley was scarce during all this time; he was gone for days. "I had his food ready, but he didn't show up to eat."

Everyone in town was terrified, but there was no place to go. The intruders would come into town, stir people up, leave town, and then in a few days return and commence harassing the townsfolk again.

Honey continued, "They did find one room, a short way from Bertie's (Grandma's) house." Opening her eyes, she pointed to a house to the right of Grandma's, on the top of a steep hill, but right in the middle of town (the house that today is owned by Larry Fresh). Others had pointed out this place but were vague about where the hidden room was located.

"The room is by the dining room; you find it soon after you go through the front door. There's a door, but it doesn't look like a door—sealed, rough wood. It's a short hall or closet; it might be under a staircase. It's on the right as you go through the door, and wooden steps lead down to the room. The door opens in."

It absolutely amazes me how all these different people, some who have never even seen or met each other, all describe, down to the minutest detail, the houses where hidden rooms are located and how access was gained to these rooms.

It was only a couple of weeks after this terrorizing started that Becky was killed. This would suggest that the Union was nervous, because the Confederacy became aware of the UGRR activities in Millboro. They probably assumed, rightly or wrongly, that Becky had told Charley about the hidden rooms and he, in turn, informed the Confederacy.

Mary Alice also mentioned the tent city that was created a few weeks after the war ended, to house the victims of the epidemic, which was probably typhoid fever.

"It was down by the river, on the town side of the bridge, on a curve in the river. The tents were on the outside curve of the river. There were two wooden bridges; the one closest to town was a foot bridge, and the carriage bridge was further down. They were made of wood with stone foundations. Anyone coming into town other than on the railroad took the bridge. I took a lot of stew out to the tent city. Sometimes there were only four or five tents but when a lot of people were sick there were as many as forty or fifty. Lots of tents and all sizes and shapes."

She continued, "When it was warm is when the most tents were there. It was spring, just before summer, when the doctors and nurses came, end of May or first of June. A lot of sick people, a lot of them died."

CHAPTER 20

JOHN JOINS THE INDIANS

WITH THE WAR OVER, the epidemic under control, and his children settled into good homes, John left Millboro and went to live with the Indians.

"I am somewhere in Virginia—I see a village, a bonfire. I am standing by the fire, with Indian men all around me. I seem to be their leader. They are dressed differently, not like typical Indians. Many wear store-bought clothes. The weather is warm, and I am wearing a leather vest and cloth pants and am barefoot. The Indians call me John; that's what the Robin's Nest Indians had always called me, too. If they saw me in town, they were to address me as John, so there would be no hint of any Indian affiliation.

I stayed with the Virginia Indians awhile, then went over to the Dakota territory and joined the "Ogala." It was part of the Sioux tribe, he said. Further checking disclosed the tribal name to be Oglala. It had been his father's tribe. He described the tribe's migration to Montana in the spring of 1876.

"All the tribe went, some in wagons, some on foot, some on horseback. We did not dare leave the women and kids behind, for fear the Union would put them onto a reservation and we would never find them again. It is taking a long time for all the various tribes to gather in and around Montana. I am riding on a horse and am alone, no family.

"After they arrived in Montana, there is a lot of fighting among the Indians, the Chiefs. They all have different ideas as to how to handle the situation. Some were for fighting. I knew the odds and tried desperately to talk them out of it. Some, like myself, wanted to continue to talk and trust the white man, even tho' we knew we could not trust him. Some were for just running and continuing to run. Some are listening to me . . . I *know* how futile it is to fight, and I still think we can negotiate with the Union. They are never going to leave us alone, but we can't win if we fight with them . . . nobody stands by what they say."

I had anticipated that John might give me a good, firsthand account of the massacre of Custer and his men, but no . . . he did not know much about the slaughter of Custer and his troops, because John, the pacifist, was elsewhere. His encampment had moved. The ones who believed what he said and did not wish to fight, moved with him. Thousands of Indians gathered in Montana.

"It was a depressing, no-win situation. I still thought we could deal with them, like I had dealt with the Union and the Confederacy. I had no trouble getting along with them, because basically they were all Americans. I feel like they can hold onto their side of the bargain, because I have been doing it all my life, and yet I am seeing that they don't. There was a lot of anger and fighting among the Indians—fist fights broke out. Some wanted to fight, some wanted to run, and some wanted to negotiate. Custer wandered into the midst of all this melee and managed to provoke them to the point where they just killed the hell out of him and his men."

Most of the group that went to Montana with him, left with him. They did not go back to the Dakotas but went on further south to some place warmer . . . to the Indian territory that is now Oklahoma. They were never on a reservation but went on to the southeast corner of the territory and set up camp outside a very small town. While in the town one day, he ran into some friends of his, white men. They were former Confederates whom he had known in Millboro.

"A whole lot of Confederates came out west after the war, and a lot of them had a great deal of money, too."

They convinced him to take the job of sheriff in the small town, and he had been happy to do so. That way, he was in a better position to take care of his family, the Indians, who had established their village near the town.

John tried very hard to recall the name of the small town in the Indian territory. It was a short name and there was an O and a P in it. This news was rather exciting, because at an earlier time, baby Peter had told of meeting with John on his way to Texas to join the Rangers. It had been in a very small town in Oklahoma, and John had been working as sheriff.

From the clues John gave me and later things that Peter said, I suspect that John may have been in a town called Boggy Depot.

He was about forty-five when he died, after he had been in the small Oklahoma town about five years. It was an accident. "I had a few acres of land on the edge of town. There is a big piece of metal, like a plow; it was stuck on something, and it broke loose, moving a stump or rock that had hung up the plow. The horses were still pulling, and it came loose suddenly, and the plow cut my leg badly. The doctor in town took care of me, but the leg became infected. Probably tetanus. I see a cut, then I see an illness, a fever, then death."

His life after he left Millboro was never very happy; it was clouded by an overwhelming sadness.

CHAPTER 21

PETER

AFTER JOHN (PAT GREENE) volunteered that he had served as a lawman and died in a small Oklahoma town, I decided to talk to Peter (Luke Gremling) again.

Early in the study, before I had even located Pat Greene, Peter stated that on his way to Texas he had encountered John working as a sheriff in a small town in Oklahoma. This observation was pretty much discounted, because John's mother Liz (Barbara Roberts) insisted he had spent the remainder of his life with the Indians.

Actually, they were both right. John said that he led the tribe to the southeast corner of the Indian territory that later became Oklahoma and, after getting them ensconced in a village a few miles out of town, he then took employment in the town. He felt he could better serve his native people through a law enforcement capacity in town.

The last time Peter saw John prior to the Oklahoma meeting was when he and Honey, who had taken him in, had gone to the Indian camp in Virginia. He had been about six years old then. John made it abundantly clear that he did not appreciate their visit, and they never tried to see him again.

Peter was just barely eighteen when he left his foster mother Honey and struck out on his own for Texas to join the Rangers. He had a horse, a bedroll, and eighteen dollars—a lot of money then. Also he had some bread and water, coffee, not a whole lot of food,

Luke Gremling was born in Orange, California.
Currently he is a firefighter for the Silent Valley Ranger Station
and attends college.
He has lived in the Elsinore area for eighteen years
and has never been to Virginia.
His role in the story is that of baby Peter,
the youngest son of Becky.

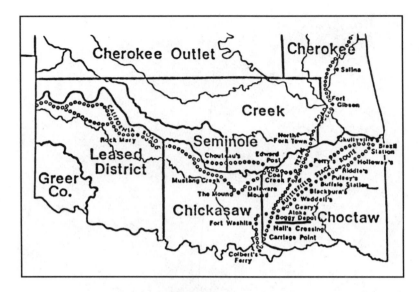

IMPORTANT ROUTES AND TRAILS

Gibson, Arrell M. *Oklahoma: A History of Five Centuries.*
2d. ed. Norman: University of Oklahoma Press, 1981.

*A map of the southeastern portion of the Indian Territory
of Oklahoma after the Civil War.
It is possible that the town of Boggy Depot was where
John was located.*

a pair of pants, a real heavy jacket, an extra shirt or two, some gloves, and long johns.

Heading east from the Richmond area, he traveled to the coast. Having never seen the ocean, he decided it was time he did. He traveled south along the coast to about where Florida is now, then cut north and west, traveling through the Alabama territory and maybe Georgia.

The town where he found John serving as marshal was very small and located in "the territory." It had no post office; mail went out on the stage. It was in the southeast part of the territory—he did not go very deeply into the territory because it belonged to the Indians and was not too safe. Peter said he passed many Indians on his journey through their territory. Some of the Indian women were the most beautiful he had ever seen but, "You wouldn't dare try to touch one of them!"

While eating in the restaurant, he heard someone mention John's name. He could scarcely believe his ears.

"They were talking about the marshal, and they said John Aushlick, and I asked them to say the name again because I thought maybe I had heard it wrong, and they said it was John Aushlick. I was really surprised, and I asked them who he was, and they said he was the marshal. I asked where his office was, and they said it was over by the stables. So, I went over there to see him. I was really kind of nervous. I wasn't sure he would want to see me, but he seemed happy I was there. He didn't recognize me when he looked at me; I looked pretty bad. I'd been traveling for a long time, was dirty, with a couple weeks growth of beard. He looked okay, was clean, a lot older, more heavyset. He looked healthy, his hair greying a little tiny bit at the temples and starting to thin out, but not much. There was a big gun at his side; it was tied down, too—it looked like he meant business. He looked like somebody I would not want to mess with."

John had assumed that Peter was just some "saddle tramp" and was very surprised when he identified himself. John's response was to inquire what in God's name Peter was doing way out there.

"I told him I was going to Texas because I wanted to be a Ranger. He looked at me and told me I was too young. My answer was—so, I would lie about my age."

Maybe it was the matter-of-fact way in which he said it but this remark struck John as very funny, and he laughed long over it, probably remembering the cavalier and audacious way he went about securing his own first job.

"So we went over to the restaurant and had some coffee and caught up on the news. I hung around town for a week or so, saw quite a bit of him during that time. He had a house a few miles from town. It was nice but not very big. A nice little garden, a couple of horses, five or six head of cattle. I spent a night or two there, but I just didn't feel right. He was gone for two or three days, dunno where he went (probably out to the Indian village). He came back a couple of days before I was going to pull out. Said I had to get moving if I was going to get to Texas before rain, before winter. It was kinda hard to leave, but I figured I would see him again once I became established, but I never did."

Peter was told about his father's accident, how he had been hurt by the plow and how the local doctor had been unable to save him. This revelation brought forth a tirade about that local doctor.

"The damn doctor in that town was a drunk; that's why he wasn't cared for properly. Drunk! He didn't know what he was doing, was half stoned most of the time. Damn drunk, didn't know what he was doing—maybe I should go back there and kill the doctor! Yeah, that doctor was a fool; think his name was Jim Taylor."

The marshal's office was just a room in the back of the stables. There was no bank in town, just a bar and a little mom and pop-type restaurant. It was mostly a cow town, a place to stop. Restaurant, bar, stables, boarding house—Miss Kate's—that's where Peter stayed when he was not with John. The general store was part of the restaurant. The town was about a day's ride into the territory from the states, fifteen or twenty miles on a good horse. There was not much of a road; it was mostly a trail. It was about a four-day ride from there into Texas. His dad was not married, but he hung around with Sue, who worked in the bar. Sue was friendly, pretty, and a working girl, very available. As there was no waitress in the bar, Sue hung out there and sometimes served drinks.

"Most of the shopkeepers, business men in town were white, a few Mexicans. There were not too many white farmers, because the Indians did not like that. The whites stayed close to the town, except when they were pushing cattle. The whites don't go too deep into the territory; if they do, they are asking for big trouble. Some people in the area have a lot of money; they come into the bar and gamble, lose a lot of money, more than I have ever seen. I met a few people while I was there. Miss Kate runs the boarding house; she had a couple of sons, one fourteen, the other younger. They kept the place pretty clean. There were two other men living there besides me. One was a lawyer; he stayed only a couple of days. The other guy, I think he may have been looking to buy some cattle. He was there when I left and had been there when I arrived. It's a good place to go if you wanted to buy cattle, a lot of people pushing them through town."

Peter remarked that he would liked to have been closer to John, but John was not like that, he was a loner. Reserved, he was the kind of person that no one could get to know very well. It was Peter's impression that, all in all, John was basically a very unhappy man.

Peter explained that John had a shell around himself, a wall. John was three-quarters Indian and had always, until he left Millboro, led a white man's life. From the time he was just a baby, it was pounded into him that he must be very quiet about his background.

Directing him to look at the Indians through the eyes of Peter, it was suggested he would fully realize how much the Indians were looked down upon, so much more than the Negroes. They were regarded as little more than animals. We cannot begin to comprehend the pecking system that prevailed then; no one today could begin to understand it.

Explosively, he replied, "Dirty! The Indians were like animals; they lived like animals. The niggers, at least they tried, they knew how to keep themselves clean!"

Before Peter departed, John admonished him not to tell anyone where he was. Peter thought the request odd and did not realize at the time that John was trying to protect his children. Had it become known that they were part Indian, or were numbered among the despised "breeds," as they were called then, they and their children would have faced social ostracism.

CHAPTER 22

RETURN TO MILLBORO I

ON OUR WAY TO MILLBORO from Washington, D.C., Maureen, Smokey, and I drove through and around the town of Staunton, Virginia, because Smokey had decided that this was the area where his old plantation house had been located. We searched to no avail, and when we were settled into the Inn in Warm Springs, I hypnotized him, handed him a map of Bath County, and with no hesitation he marked a spot off the main road between Warm Springs and Millboro, a little less than half way down the hill near Bath Alum Springs.

When Samuel's plantation had been there, no other houses were close by, and he owned a great deal of the adjoining countryside. However, at the present time, there are a lot of homes built along the highway. Smokey found it all very confusing and finally asked me to hypnotize him again, which I did. Immediately he pointed to a large clearing under a span of high trees, in a meadow behind the houses that fronted the highway. Some of the local residents showed us how to get over the high fence that protected the pastureland and said it would be all right for us to walk back there, as they were friends of the family who owned the property, and they felt comfortable in granting us permission.

We walked for a long time over the land and decided, from obvious signs, it was home to both horses and cows. Finally we arrived at the clearing and found that no overt signs of the old house remained, but we discovered several old bricks and pieces of glazed tile, which indicated that a building had once stood there.

Smokey had made a sketch of the mansion earlier, and we could mentally picture how the old plantation had looked, stately and commanding, nestled there among the trees.

Returning to the car, we headed in the direction of Millboro. As we turned left onto the main highway, Smokey let out a yelp of surprise and hollered, "It's my bridge; there's my bridge I used to cross on my way to Millboro!"

Much earlier in the story, Samuel had told how he rode his horse down the road to the main highway, then crossed a bridge, turned left on a small road immediately after the bridge, went up over the hill, and came down into Millboro. Even though the going was a little bit rough, it was a much shorter and more direct way into town. He always went that way, except when driving his large wagon (in which he hauled guns and any other contraband he could get his hands on).

Today the bridge is in very bad shape and is definitely out of commission. Smokey was absolutely ecstatic over finding it, and I took several photos of him standing on "his" bridge. The road, just beyond the bridge, on which he used to travel, is still there and runs off to the left, presumably in the direction of Millboro.

Larry Fresh, the realtor in town who had helped me find the owner of "Grandma's" property, met us in Millboro, and we went through a house he owns in town, close to Grandma's place. This house shows up clearly in the old picture of the town—to the right of Grandma's house, on top of a steep hill. Several persons had pointed to that house and claimed it contained a very small hidden room. Baby Peter had said, "In the house that the realtor owns, the room is entered through a closet."

Entering through the back door, we walked from room to room in the empty house. Smokey, hypnotized, led me immediately through the living room and into a short closet off to one side. We had to stoop down to get into it. He explained that the back wall of the closet had swung outward to make a door; one stepped through the door and made a sharp right turn, then went down two or three

Smokey studies "Samuel's" bridge.

A sketch that Smokey drew of Samuel's old plantation house.
The small house to right is where the household slaves lived.
The porch-type balconies on front of house were called
a "widow's walk."

The area where Samuel's plantation house once stood.

Old Millboro in the 1800s.
X marks Grandma's house. O marks Larry's house.

Larry's house today.

Closet in Larry's house, said to be the entrance to a hidden room.

A large lot next to the Millboro firehouse, which once held a large stone house.

"Cistern" cover on the lot today.

"Cistern" lid lifts up to show that the area has been filled in.

steps into a very small room. The area where the room is located would be directly under a stairwell, as Honey had suggested. Later, we went into the basement of the house, which is unfinished. The flooring of the house is overhead, dirt underfoot, and all four walls are fairly open. However, in the area under the stairwell, the dirt rises up to the underside of the house. This has to be where the room is, or was. My people say that the room has been filled in with rocks and sludge. There was no tunnel leading into the cubicle, but there was an exit of some sort, allowing egress into the back yard. It is generally concurred by the people in the study that the abolitionists in Millboro "gave" this room to the Confederates, most likely because there were no tunnels leading into it, and therefore it would not expose the other rooms in town. Seemingly, the ploy worked, as it appears the Rebels gave up the search for hidden rooms after finding and exposing this one.

From Larry's house, Smokey, in a trance as Samuel, led me in a direct line to where the old stone house had stood, gazing back over his left shoulder from time to time to get his bearings.

Larry had said that he thought the old stone house would had to have stood where the Millboro fire station is now located. However, Smokey, without a moment's hesitation, led me in a straight, unwavering path up to a very large lot adjacent to the firehouse. The next day, we borrowed a probe from the owner of "Grandma's" property and, with the owner's permission, bored down into the soil where Smokey claimed the room was. We went down about one-and-a-half feet and hit an impenetrable object. All we brought up was a whitish, resin type of material. We probed in several places and hit the same obstacle. Banging the probe up and down several times, it made a dull, thumping sound, and we were convinced we were hitting the wooden ceiling of a hidden room.

Later, it was stated by another participant that the Indians had coated the wooden beams with a white, resin-like material to preserve them.

The chamber, according to most in the group, is very large, about twelve feet by twelve feet, the largest in the Millboro area. According to Smokey, it is not intact, as some parts of the sides have caved in, as have the tunnels. Parts of it were filled in with a grey, clay-like stuff. Peter had claimed that there were no supporting walls in that chamber, just the wooden plank ceiling.

Because there were no walls, the owners used to dig tunnels out of the room in which to hide things. They buried bodies, guns, and anything incriminating they had to get rid of, then they sealed them over with the dirt. Peter had stated, "There is stuff buried on all sides of that room!"

On one side of the property, towards the firehouse, is a large, concrete cover. It looked to be about two feet by three feet in size. The cover lifts up and exposes, about a foot down, a lot of gray concrete or clay material. The walls of the hole have been lined with concrete, and obviously it has been filled in. When the owner of the property was asked what this cistern-like object was, she replied that she thought it had something to do with the septic system. Smokey claimed it was one of the entrances into the room, and its location would have been correct, from what I have been told. Later I located, in an old archaeological journal, a reference to this concrete, box-like entrance to Indian rooms.

One of my primary goals on this visit to Millboro was to locate another old house that had underground rooms or tunnels. In his very earliest regressions, Pat Greene (John) mentioned several times a large white house, about one-half to one mile out of town, which stood high on a hill over the railroad tracks. He said, "I can see the slaves jumping off the train and running up the hillside to the old house where they would be hidden."

We drove paralleling the railroad for about a mile and located a large residence, on a hill. Because the house has been so beautifully cared for and is in such excellent condition, we doubted it was the place. However, further research has proven that it is.

Today it is called the old Cauthorn house, and it is owned and inhabited by Anna Cauthorn, whose late husband was descended from the original builders.

Most of the credit for helping me pinpoint the house and establishing its history goes to Mr. Harry Jolly of Burlington, North

Carolina. Mr. Jolly's mother was a Bratton, and he is a cousin by marriage to Anna Cauthorn.

Mr. Townley Cauthorn came to Millboro around 1850, when the railroad was built. He married Martha Bratton who, upon her father's death, inherited one-half of the Bratton land. The young couple built a log cabin on the property, and later built the eight-room frame house that stands there today.

Both the Bratton and Cauthorn families were, and still are, active in the Millboro Presbyterian Church, which stood a couple of lots above Grandma's house, and which was the unofficial headquarters for the Underground Railroad activity in the town.

Mr. Jolly had asked me to convey his regards to Anna Cauthorn on one of my trips to Millboro. Anna was hard to catch at home, but her charming daughter graciously showed me around the place.

The original basement (there is a later addition next to it) did not look as though there could be any place for a hidden room. However, as we looked around the property, the daughter pointed out the area behind the house where the slave quarters had stood, on into the 20th century. One old wooden shed, still standing and in surprisingly good condition, had housed a black employee, descended from the Cauthorn slaves, until his demise a few years ago.

Lenette (Sally) had been with me during the visit to the Cauthorn house. Later, under hypnosis as Sally, she described the wooden shacks, or slave quarters, behind the house. "About four or five, kind of scattered, two or three feet apart. The underground room is a couple of feet in back of the last shack. A lot of trees and shrubs hiding the entrance." She finished by adding that there is concrete over the entrance today.

Barbara Roberts (Liz) had stated much earlier in this story that immediately after the war's end, the Union had sent soldiers into Bath County to seal off all the hidden rooms, in order to protect the abolitionists from their neighbors, many of whom blamed the Underground Railroad for the South's defeat in the war. Others have said that most of the entrances are sealed over with concrete, except for the basement of the Green Valley farm, in which an entire brick wall was erected.

CHAPTER 23

RETURN TO MILLBORO II

IN THE FALL OF 1993, Lynn, Evie, and I journeyed to Millboro. As we walked about the area, Evie functioned under a double handicap. She was walking either on crutches or a cane, recovering from extensive surgery on an ankle. Her second, more unique obstacle, was that she was functioning and being directed by both Roy Farmer and Running Springs.

The year previous, when Maureen, Smokey, and I had been in the area, I had enjoyed a rather lengthy discussion with the minister of the Williamsville Presbyterian church. His rapt interest in my work seemed very sincere. From him I understood that the church owned all the land that ran up the hill behind the chapel. At that time I inquired if there would be a problem if we poked about on the church grounds. My plan had been to borrow Charlie Williams' metal probe and explore the yard near the rear of the church, to see if we could discover the roof of a buried room. His answer to me was, "Poke around to your heart's content, and if you discover anything interesting, be sure to let me know." Unfortunately, time ran out before we could carry out that mission.

When we parked in front of the old church a year later, I hoped to carry out a more in-depth investigation.

As we strolled about the churchyard, I noticed that the pipe that had been protruding from the area where we think the buried room is, was missing . . . simply no longer there.

Suddenly Evie firmly ordered, "Follow me!" and started pell mell up the heavily wooded hill behind the church. It was all I could do to keep up with her. The terrain is very steep, densely covered with trees. The ground and fallen leaves were wet and slippery from a recent rain, and the going was extremely difficult.

Totally disregarding her painfully injured ankle, Evie clamored up the hillside, excited beyond description. Face flushed, eyes a little wild, and breathing hard, she called back to me, "Running Springs is leading me to something up here!!"

A few moments later, as I labored to join her, she hollered, "Mom, I think I have found the mouth to the tunnel!"

Out of breath and exhausted, I caught up with her and saw what certainly could be the mouth of a tunnel. It appeared to be man-made. It was a small hole or opening in the hillside, covered over by what appeared to be a carefully placed log. The terrain was not such that it would lend itself to a natural cave, and it was much too contrived-appearing to have been engineered by a wild animal. We decided to borrow a shovel and later probe it further.

There was no cemetery or burial plot on the hill behind the church. Evie pointed off in a southeasterly direction and claimed, "Roy and Martha are buried on a hilltop over there." Later investigation proved her right.

Local people pointed the way to a small, family hilltop cemetery, not far from the church. They stated that the public was welcome to visit the burial plot anytime, and that it would necessitate crossing a suspension bridge. One very charming, handsome young man, dressed in hunting togs, even offered to lead us to the suspension bridge. When I inquired if I would be able to drive across the bridge he, deadly serious, answered, "Oh, no Ma'am, I wouldn't advise you to try to drive across that bridge."

When we saw the bridge, we all doubled over with laughter. It was about two-and-a-half feet wide and would not have accommodated even a kiddie car.

Then another problem arose. Both Lynn and Evie are phobic about heights, especially when those heights are swaying back and forth in the breeze like a hammock. Lynn summed it up succinctly

*The area where the girls said
Roy and Martha's farmhouse stood.*

*A concrete bridge that Lynn claimed used to be made of wood,
a bridge that the Indians used frequently.*

*The Windy Cove Presbyterian Church in Millboro Springs,
built in the early 1700s. Note the different types of brick
used in adding rooms to the original structure over the years.*

*Alley between the old bank building in Millboro and a shed
next to the boarding house. Notice the concrete patch.
Evie claims there is an underground room,
or kiva, under the patch.*

Williamsville Presbyterian Church today.

Presbyterian Church above "Grandma's" house in Millboro today.

Bath House in Warm Springs, Virginia

A chair built especially for Mrs. Robert E. Lee in the women's bath house in Warm Springs

Old Marshall cemetery in Williamsville

Evie sits among the broken headstones.

*Possible opening
to tunnel leading
to room under
Williamsville
Presbyterian
Church*

*Suspension
bridge over
Cowpasture
River*

Lynn and Evie pose on suspension bridge.

by announcing, "There's no way on God's earth you are going to get me to walk over that bridge!"

Using the same ploy I had applied a few weeks earlier to get Maureen onto an airplane to fly east to appear on a T.V. show, I put both girls into a trance. They were then instructed that the part of their mind that caused them to be uncomfortable about walking on the bridge would remain asleep. Counting to three instead of five, they were told that they would open their eyes, be partially out of the trance, and would follow me across the bridge, which they did like little lambs. When we reached solid ground on the other side, I continued counting . . . three . . . four . . . five, you are now wide awake and fully conscious. It worked like a charm, both coming and going. The road swerved off to the right, then circled left following the river. After walking about one-half of a mile, we spotted a very steep hill, dotted with headstones, off to our left.

Fighting our way through thick underbrush and brambles up the very steep hill, we wondered how in tarnation they ever got a heavy, body-filled casket up there to bury it. A study of the headstones showed many members of the Marshall family to be buried there, along with several other family names. No Farmer or, as Roy had suggested, possibly Farmier or Formier. Evie said that Roy and Martha, Eve, and son Matthew, had been buried at the very top of the hill. When we reached the spot we found the remains of four broken or shattered headstones. Later, in the trance, Roy said that some member of the family, possibly a Marshall, had a serious falling out with one of Roy's surviving sons and, after drinking heavily, he took a large mallet and deliberately destroyed the headstones. It certainly appeared as though something of this nature had happened.

On the way back to Warm Springs, we passed beautiful pasture land that the girls said had been Roy's farm. It now appears to be part of the Green Valley Farm. A short way down the road, Lynn suddenly called out, pointing, "There's the old wooden bridge the Indians used to come over." Closer inspection showed that what had probably once been a wooden bridge was now made of concrete. Evidently, the road that crossed that bridge had, a hundred and fifty years ago, led to an Indian village. Lynn said Martha frequently hired Indians to help her around the farm, especially after Roy had been injured, paying them with milk and eggs.

One day was spent looking around Robin's Nest. We searched in vain for the large white rock, but failed to locate it. We are certain it is up there, however, because all the Indians and several of the white people in the group have talked about the white rock. It was a definite landmark in the Indian community. What searching we did was slowed down and thwarted by Evie's injured ankle.

Tromping through woods and over hills and valleys in the Virginia countryside can be extremely exhausting, and several times we welcomed a late afternoon soak in the hot sulphur baths in Warm Springs. The bath houses are large, circular buildings. First built was the man's bathhouse, erected in the 1700s, and later, in the early 1800s, the women's house was built. We were fascinated by the special chair that had been constructed in the women's bathhouse for Mrs. Robert E. Lee, who suffered incapacitating rheumatism for a large part of her life.

Made of wood, the chair is suspended over a special well in the bath house. A series of pulleys and levers are arranged that lowered her, chair and all, into the water.

One day, we walked down the road that ran directly above the hole we had found. While poking about in what we believed to be the mouth of a tunnel leading down through the hill into a hidden room under the church, we were suddenly accosted by a thoroughly irate property owner. It seems we were unknowingly trespassing on his property. First, he threatened to have us arrested, then jailed, and there was even talk of shooting us. Our explanation that we thought we were on church property, with permission, fell on deaf ears. Apparently the church owns only the property half way up the hill . . . at least, according to him.

Our plans called for us to meet with some archaeologists from Tennessee the following Saturday. When we asked the furious property owner if we might be allowed to bring the scientists to the site, the answer was an unwavering, "Absolutely not!!"

A hundred years ago, if a Southern property owner had reacted this way to a stranger wandering a few feet onto his property, one might have suspected he was manufacturing illegal moonshine nearby. This is the second site we have been prohibited from entering . . . first the Green Valley Farm, whose owners have no desire to cooperate in this research, and now the hill behind the Williamsville church. Certainly, when people buy property on which to retire, they are legally and morally entitled to privacy and protection from invasive eyes. But when they are keeping from the world and posterity, artifacts and locations of great interest and historical significance, it seems reasonable that archaeologists and anthropologists should at least be allowed to peruse the site. One has to wonder why the owners of these colorful old locations feel threatened by society.

On Saturday we went to the Millboro General store to meet with the team of archaeologists from Tennessee. I took them (with the owner's permission) to the lot next to the fire station and showed them the concrete, box-like structure that has been attributed to Indian kivas. We had hoped to probe down with a metal shaft (as we had done the year before) to hit the wooden roof below, but because Charlie Williams, the owner of the property under Grandma's house, had failed to keep his appointment with us, we had no probe to use.

Some of us then walked about the area of Robin's Nest. The archaeologists were intrigued by a huge, circular, cleared area about a half-mile from what I feel was the living area of the village. It certainly does appear to have been a meeting and ceremonial center.

A couple of months prior to this trip to Millboro, Evie had casually stated one day, "There's a buried room, or kiva, near the old boarding house, but they have paved over it."

From this revelation I assumed that the room, if there was one, was in front of the boarding house, and the asphalt road was built over it. However, while we were walking about near the general store, Evie grabbed my arm and pointed to an alley running between the old brick bank building and a small wooden shed right next to the boarding house. For the first six to eight feet, the alley consists of dirt, with grass growing in the center. Then, for about another six or seven feet, is a rectangular, concrete slab. The remainder of the alley is dirt, like the first part. According to Evie, the room under the slab is very old. It was not used to hide slaves, because the settlers were unaware it was there. It was sealed up hundreds of years ago, and even the later Indians were unaware of its existence.

Presumably, it was paved over because, due to foot and horse traffic, wagons, and later heavy trucks, the roof timbers gave way and either caved in or bowed, causing an inconvenient dip in the earth's surface. Someone poured concrete into the abyss to level off the alley. Later, Honey was quizzed regarding the small red building next to the boarding house. "It was my wash room; we hauled the water into the shed in buckets. The floor was cement or brick; it sloped a little, and the water ran out a drain and onto the yard next to the building." This would have been directly over where the room is supposed to be located, and probably all that water, over enough years, helped deteriorate the wooden ceiling of the room.

Everyone in this group who visits the Millboro area reacts in an emotional way. When Maureen and Joe visited the area, the ambience was one of unconcealed anticipation and excitement. When Barbara Roberts went back with me a year later, it was an emotion-filled experience. Tears coursed down her face a great deal of the time, especially when we were in the area of Robin's Nest.

During another trip with Smokey and Maureen, Smokey was highly charged throughout the visit, leading us from pillar to post, and absolutely refusing to quit until we had located Bratton's Bridge.

Throughout the trip with Lynn and Evie, Lynn was strangely silent a large part of the time, as she related to the lifetime of Martha, especially as we drove around Williamsville. Evie, however, had a stronger reaction than anyone had previously. She was torn, wherever we went, between Roy and Running Springs. The effect on her was much the same as my reaction one time when I did psychic work with law-enforcement officers while visiting a murder site. Evie was unable to keep food down and had a lot of trouble sleeping. Her statement was that there was so much stimuli wherever we went that she was in a constant state of agitation. She remained in this state of "psychic burnout" until we left the Millboro area and returned to California.

CHAPTER 24

THE SUBJECTS DISCUSS
UNDERGROUND ROOMS

BECAUSE LUKE (PETER) has proven to be fairly unerring in his instincts regarding this Millboro story, I quizzed him regarding the room reported to be next to Honey's wash house. He stated that a couple of times baby Peter had tried to play in the water coming out of the wash house, until Honey had caught him. The concrete was not there, in the alley, then; it was just dirt. He felt the concrete had been poured there around 1935 and was put there because of the water that had been poured into the alley for so long. It had caused the roof of the room to bow, creating a depression in the alley. The room under the concrete is very deteriorated, he said, and may contain human bones and Indian pottery. There may also be petroglyphs on the walls.

My last trip to Millboro was made with Lenette (Sally). While we were sitting in front of the general store, she pointed across the tracks and said, "There's something over there . . . I keep sensing something in the brush. There's something under there, where they used to stay . . . a room."

Several times John mentioned to me that there was a small room across the railroad tracks, right in the center of town, a place where slaves hid until they could get to one of the regular rooms. Sally called it a "holding pen."

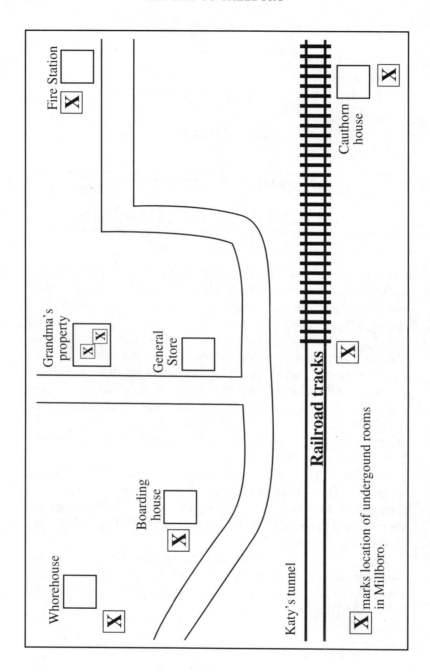

Fire Station

Grandma's property

General Store

Boarding house

Whorehouse

Cauthorn house

Railroad tracks

Katy's tunnel

X marks location of undergound rooms in Millboro.

According to Samuel, it is a small room and will hold about six people. The door is covered with sod and dirt. "People walk over it all the time and never see it." Lenette had mentioned that the room was near a boat. Smokey concluded, "There's an old boat, a bass boat, today, near the room." This statement surprised me. Lenette had mentioned a boat, which we immediately located. She is the only one of the group who has been in that area and actually seen the boat.

When I questioned Evie, she said that the small room is across the tracks from the general store. Then she shocked me by asking: "Is there a boat? I see a silver metal boat."

All three agreed that the room was located near the boat that now sits on the property. They also agreed that because roads have been cut into the area and bulldozers have rearranged dirt, the room may now be deeper than it was in the days of slavery.

It was during my fifth trip, this time with Lenette, that I was made aware of the change in attitude of many of the residents of Millboro toward this research. Until that trip the local people were exceptionally friendly and helpful in our quest to unearth the past. We all learned to love the sweet, friendly people of Millboro.

Imagine my shock when I received a phone call one night in my motel room during my last trip. A terse, masculine voice informed me in no uncertain terms that I and my people were unwelcome in Millboro, and it would be better for all concerned if we left and did not return.

Looking back on events leading up to the phone call, I should have been aware of a change in the attitude of the locals. First, the owner of Grandma's property had failed to meet with me when I had a team of archaeologists prepared to enter the rooms under Grandma's property, after fervently agreeing to meet with us. Also, the young couple who own the lot next to the fire station success-fully avoided me, refusing to answer the door when I went to their house. The owner of the property above the church, where we had located the tunnel mouth had threatened me with jail for being on his property. When I wrote to the Presbyterian Church in Wil-liamsville requesting permission to roll back a small corner of the carpeting to locate the trap door leading to the hidden room, I received a firm, curt NO!

The owner of the boarding house sent me a letter granting me unlimited permission to dig anywhere I choose, under or around the concrete patch. Yet, when I went to do so, he had carefully parked his pickup truck directly over the concrete, making excavation impossible. I also received a terse note from the owner of the Cauthorn property stating they had "no interest" in unearthing any hidden room.

This radical change in attitude toward my work shocked and distressed me. Finally, a long term resident of Bath County, whom I have known for several years and who is sympathetic and excited by this research, explained to me, "The people here know full well that there are underground rooms and tunnels where you say there are. A few wealthy and vocal retirees have convinced the locals that, should these underground rooms be exposed by archaeologists, swarms of tourists, especially *black* tourists, will overrun the area, wanting to see where Grandma and Grandpa hid while they were escaping slavery. This scares the hell out of them!"

My informant ended by stating that there was also a large subculture in the County that is furious over what is happening and would like to see the rooms exposed for the recognition and eventual prosperity it would bring to the area.

I was also told that the local people are terrified that bulldozers would come in and tear the town apart. Evidently, they fail to realize that archaeologists do not work that way. The area where Robin's Nest once stood is currently owned by the U.S. government. My people tell me that the land atop the hill is rife with underground kivas and other remnants of an earlier culture. Perhaps in time, archaeologists will discover a rewarding dig up there.

It was suggested that I try to document Millboro's role in the Underground Railroad. People who think this is possible fail to understand the danger in keeping records of any kind concerning the Underground Railroad. The book, *Harriet Tubman,* by Bently, describes how a black man named William Still maintained the "office" of the Philadelphia Vigilance Committee to assist runaways. He attempted to get them food, clothing, shelter, and perhaps news of relatives who had come North earlier. Mr. Still, at that time kept extensive records, with the hope of reuniting families. After the Slave Act of 1850 was passed, many people destroyed any records that had been kept. Later, when Sam Brown, a white abolitionist who urged slaves to rise up against their masters, was executed, strong anti-black sentiment prevailed and record-keeping became even more dangerous. William Still hid what records he had in a graveyard.

In his comprehensive book, *The Underground Railroad: From Slavery to Freedom* (MacMillan, 1899), Wilbur Siebert states that because of the danger of stringent reprisal, little information concerning any part of the Underground Road was allowed to get into print. He mentions that Robert Purvis of Philadelphia kept a record of the fugitives who passed through his hands until the trepidation of his family after the Slave Act passed caused him to destroy it. Siebert also describes how Daniel Gibbons of Columbia, Pennsylvania, kept a detailed record of the slaves he assisted. He entered the name of the slave's master, the fugitive's name and age, and any new name he took. Eventually the record book developed into a large volume. Immediately after the Slave Act passed, he methodically burned the incriminating evidence that would have brought disaster upon him had it ever been discovered. As Roy put it so passionately, "We could lose everything!"

Maureen displays dresses she made for her baby
without a pattern, as Becky used to.
Her homemade soap is on the sofa.

CHAPTER 25

MAUREEN MEETS BECKY

THE FOLLOWING ACCOUNT by Maureen Williamson not only describes how the entire saga of Millboro got its start, but also provides a firsthand account of the mental and emotional journey—at times challenging—concomitant to the process of recalling memories of past-life experiences.

"Through the mist you were there
    and coming to me
with my name on your lips
and my smile in your eyes.
    I hurried toward you,
      my heart in my hands,
      my allness to offer,
my heart for your prize. . . ."

That may have been how this started. Glimpses into a misty past that filtered down through many layers of my consciousness, becoming the contraction of muscles leading to my writing hand that, in turn, became the ink flowing through my pen and onto the page.

Maybe.

But whatever its genesis, the feelings that followed my recollections of Becky's life lived in Civil War Virginia were to become far more than filtered layers, muscle contractions, and flowing ink. These experiences are tangible, intricate, compelling, and alive.

They are not simple memories, nor are they figments of desire. This is real, this is Becky, and this is a record of me. This is not the remainder or reminder of Becky, but a wonderful, wondrous part of me, Maureen. And I love this story.

I first came to Dr. Marge Rieder, hypnotherapist, in 1987 at the direction of a mutual friend. I'd come to enlist Dr. Rieder's help in remembering a childhood incident, and it had been suggested to me that hypnosis was commonly and easily employed to retrieve lost memories. With that in mind, I gave it a try. I took to hypnosis structure well and did, in fact, recover what memories I'd lost. However, it seemed that hypnosis had also recovered memories of whose existence I was never aware. These "memories" held great interest for me, and I was prompted to pursue them further.

Having never been exposed to the concepts of reincarnation, other than casually, I was taken off guard by the story that crossed my hypnotized lips as I relayed the life and times of one Rebeccah Ashford (aka Ailstock). Out of the trance, I recall stating that this was indeed a most interesting situation in development, and I would be hard put not to investigate it further. If I could document where this odd tale was coming from, I would feel quite good.

I had no qualms about the notion of accepting a universal-type ESP: perhaps sound-wave energy was being received by the electrical circuitry of my brain. I'd been informed that sound waves never die, so this was a possible easy explanation. Or maybe this was a brand of genetic memory, or it could have been the script to a long-ago-seen film, or maybe I'd read a book someplace about this woman. I set out documenting by hauling out the encyclopedia and looking up Virginia. There were no Ashfords in there, but there was a small dot of a town that fit the basic description and area that I'd seen in regression. Dr. Rieder and I went to work from there. After several weeks of regression and research, I concluded that I could not disprove that my memories were coming from somewhere other than what I had seen or read about. I began to accept that I had perhaps been here before, that I could have been truly remembering an earlier time for me, and if I was really doing that, I was doing it 130 years later.

One afternoon in 1987, several months into our sessions, I was leaving my friend/regressionist's office, when I stopped my car in the middle of the avenue leading to the outside street. I sat behind the wheel and felt the sensation of waves generating from the bottom of me to the top, and I felt them rolling back down. This is fear, I informed myself. This is fear, and I am scared, because I do not know what to call this very real thing that has me stopped in the avenue. I cannot give this thing a name and identify it, so that I can define its boundaries, begin to understand it, and put it in the correct cabinet. And I can't get the hell rid of Becky, either. I felt like two people struggling to be heard. Becky was dancing around Maureen's mind, and Maureen was running like crazy to get away from this very familiar stranger. I sat there for some fifteen minutes attempting to categorize the sessions, the research I'd put in. I tried to integrate the two persons into one physical person and came away feeling that, confusing as this was, integrate is what I must do. Having invested several months into this work already, I had one thing left to do with this, which was to accept it as a very real, physical part of my life. I decided to make a friend out of Becky and to categorize this as a part of my past, as I'd done with the balance of my childhood and adolescent memories. All of my other memories had their proper place in my past, and so would these. I figured to drive myself home just then. Of course, all this transpired during the light of day, where there were no shadows. But the nights were a whole different story.

Sleep, in the early days of my regression, was often troubled. Hours were endless some nights, while on other nights, sleep barely came. I had dreams and some of those dreams caused me to write poems that I did not fully understand. Some of the dreams were filmy and pleasant, some were most uncomfortable. But all of them made me think. At night, in sleep, I would "meet," for the first time, people I already knew, and some who I still do not know. But the familiar faces looked different in my sleep from how they looked in the daylight. Our clothing was unlike what we wear now. Our relationships were different, too, yet they were still the same. These dreams would come in bits too thready to create a sequence that I could recognize as a workable picture, one that I could recognize in the daylight. I felt comfort, safety, and happiness in some of them and, in others, I felt confusion, even fear. I was afraid, because I did not know if I was dreaming or remembering, and if I was remembering, why wasn't I doing that while I was awake?

One dream begins with a bright, clear day, yet I am cold. There are white filmy things blowing around me, and I hear a young baby crying. I see a battered wooden box, a rope of some sort, and the transparent face of a man, covered with a dark beard. The baby cries, and I begin to spiral down and down and down, past rough planks of wood fastened by square nails. I smell hay, sweet and wet, and I can't breathe real well. I feel scared, but it's not really a nightmare. I see some green and a lot of black while I'm spiraling, and I see red, too. I don't understand the colors or why they should be there while I'm swirling. The baby is still crying, I'm still spiraling, I still see the red and the black, and I still smell the hay. I wonder why I'm falling, what are those colors; I know I'm dizzy now; shouldn't I be standing, and where the hell is that baby's mum? I wake up with all my blankets and sheets pulled apart. I'm sweating, and it's not really warm this time of year. I'm awake and then I realize that what I have here are the brittle bones of memory, which have in them a breathing marrow that is flowing into the living bones of my present. I know this now.

Becky was murdered in her barn one afternoon as she was hanging out her laundry, with one baby clinging to her skirt and another hiding in the barn, when Becky's bearded murderer approached. Of course her baby cried. The black was her faint, the red was the blood she saw through her dying eyes, and the baby was Becky's own.

Although I had previously decided on integration and friendship with Becky, following through on a full-time basis was difficult, as this was not an experience whose realness I could touch or taste or test. I simply had to accept my doubts and questions and try to understand. It comforted me to know that I still possessed the ability to question. It gave me concrete evidence of comprehension and of my own sanity. If I had the good sense to question, I must still have a good grip on myself, and if I had that, then I could accept the past. The problem was that the past had become very present.

In the midst of these excavations, though, was a great sense of excitement, the thrill of discovering an enigma that I did not really understand. Becky was fast becoming a friend as I continued to excavate. I learned many things from her, many of them practical, such as making soap. I was raised in the California beach communities, so it follows that soap-making would not have been a project I would have undertaken. Yet, through her, I learned how to produce lovely, rich bars of soap that is actually quite congenial to the skin. Since my soap production is on a smaller scale than Becky's was, I am able to improvise and elaborate on the original formula, with additions of lavender flowers, crushed sage, and oatmeal. As a matter of fact, Dr. Rieder uses only Becky's soap, and I don't use any others, either.

Sewing clothes from scratch and making patterns was another skill I learned from Becky, who went into great detail about the techniques through hypnosis. In putting those directions into practice, I was able to build some cunning little dresses and bonnets for my daughter, Caitlin. And I have learned to "swim one chicken through three suppers," which is quite a feather in the cap of a "beach girl."

Discovering the people with whom Becky had related 130 years ago would take volumes to describe. The word I have to use here is *spellbinding,* as many of these people were not strangers. Some were related intimately and some more casually, which gave me cause to suspect that something less metaphysical than my first ideas might be afoot. In my research, though, I discovered that it would be highly unusual to regress into a life that contained no familiar souls. Some of these familiar meetings were provocative, others were comical, and all of them were fascinating. Several instances stand out in my mind as more impressive, and one of these was with Diana Lovegren. Diana was Becky's young daughter, Elizabeth, and my first meeting with her provoked a motherly command to "get a sweater on you, because it's cold out today." Diana is a bit older than me, so our surprise at my directive was evident. I felt strong maternal instincts around her that did not seem inappropriate.

My first meeting in this life with my husband, Smokey, was an odd one as well. We attended the same function one evening, and after we'd been introduced, I noticed myself looking over towards him more often than I felt I had a reason to. He was a little older than I, and if I had been in the market for a man, it would not have been an obviously "earthy" man, as Smokey is. Little did I know that three years later I would become Mrs. Smokey.

Millie Sproule, a lovely woman who has been like a mother to me for some seventeen years, also had a prominent place in Civil War Millboro. Of all the people in this project I would have expected myself to recognize without hypnosis, it would have been this woman. If I had depended on that expectation and bet the rent on it, I would have had to move. I would have clearly tagged her to be Becky's mum, but she was actually the proprietress of the town's boarding house, the same boarding house where Becky had frequent trysts with her lover.

The relationship I have with my son, Luke, had always been close and warm. This is normally so between mothers and sons; however, with Luke, I had a greater compulsion toward keeping him safe. Luke had indicated that he had, until the regressions, held an unaccountable fear that harm would come to me. I had been burdened with a similar fear that Luke could be orphaned, and then who's to look after him? It did not come as a great shock to discover who Becky's crying babe in the barn had been.

Perhaps the most intriguing response I've displayed so far has to be my initial reaction to meeting Pat Greene, who had been Becky's husband, John. We first met at a party to celebrate the publication of Marge's (Dr. Rieder's) book, *Mission to Millboro*. After being introduced to Pat, I spotted Millie across the room and immediately bundled my small daughter to Pat with the words, "Will you hold her for a minute?" Then I bounced across the room. Seconds later, I realized what I had done, slunk back to fetch my child, and was stricken with instant, profound humiliation. I am a most protective mother and would no more leave my infant with a total stranger than I would strip naked and cha-cha through the streets. By handing my baby over the way I did, I perhaps came closer to "being" Becky than I would ever have dreamed possible.

Perhaps these influences from the past churn far deeper than I suspect.

After a year had elapsed since the start of our Millboro study, Marge decided the time had come to take a trip across the country to see if any of this information gleaned through hypnosis had a factual base. An exciting year had just passed that was full of adventure, discovery, and hours pouring over libraries of books and mountains of audio tapes. If this saga was going to give birth to any truth, the only place left to search for it was in Millboro, Virginia.

Marge, Joe Nazarowski, and I left Los Angeles one day in May to set foot on Virginia soil that evening.

Joe bore the name of Charley during the Civil War, though he was referred to as Peter, by Becky, and had been one of Becky's lovers. She always held him in high regard, not feeling threatened by him in any way, so it was no surprise that Joe's and my friendship had always been a comfortable one. On that vein, I did also discover that the nature of one's past life relationship did not mean that one identical to it would be resumed upon a subsequent lifetime, which was an interesting note, I thought. However, I observed that the warmth and the trust in this case provided a gentle foundation from one life into the next, as would a life colored by anger or mistrust, no doubt.

Our landing in Lynchburg, Virginia, was a monumental launching into the physical presence of Becky's life. I could have in no way prepared myself for that impact. After we left the tarmac to await our luggage at the small airfield, I surveyed my surroundings in an almost time-warped manner. It seemed as though I was suspended, somehow. I saw in the distance a shade of green on the trees, that rich, bright, almost iridescent shade of green that I had responded to so many times during my life. That shade is particular, not one often seen in California, and one that, if I did see it on some fleeting dusk, would provoke deep senses of peace, fulfillment, and even joy. I held off alone near the tarmac while Marge and Joe collected the baggage, and I drank it in. I recall tears. I do not recall speaking to anyone, nor would it have been possible for me to speak, if I actually could have thought of anything to say. This was my moment, and at that time, I don't think I was a selfless enough person to want to share it. Just then, I staked a claim to Becky's turf, and Maureen returned home to a home she'd never seen.

I can't elaborate too much on what I expected to find in Millboro; I recall only that I feared to find fear, perhaps due to Becky's life having been taken from her so early. Maybe I feared the unknown, who knows now? If I had jotted down notes previous to our arrival, I doubt seriously that what I found there would have matched them.

We very nearly drove right through Millboro our first time through. Joe and I were peering out the car windows, knowing full well that we'd see precisely what we'd known we'd find there, but we sailed right through! Then we spied a home that looked familiar, yet it wasn't where we remembered it to be. It should have been just outside of town and on the right, which is exactly where it was—except that we'd driven right past the town, which looked nothing like it had the last time we'd been there. Of course it didn't . . . over 100 years had passed! When we got our bearings, our senses uncurled slowly, at first, then developed an independent volition. We were suddenly surrounded by the taste and the touch of Millboro, as it had been. It felt like a single violin, at first, a solitary string, which gradually resonated in harmony with more strings, as we explored, step by step, through the town. The strings built on each other, feeding and swelling, until they grew to such fullness that a wonderful, ecstatic crescendo issued forth from that one violin that had waited 130 years to be heard once again.

I was home!

Marge would place me in what she calls a walking trance, having me see from two perspectives simultaneously. From this vantage point, it didn't take long to direct our troop to the site of my old house. It no longer stood, but in its place a lovely, tall Baptist church graced the grounds. What a marvelous replacement, I thought. I was overcome, it seems, by a myriad of memories, emotions, hopes. However, I was not prepared to be humbled as I was. We strolled the grounds; I pointed out the clearing where Becky had made her soap and showed off the remains of a feed box John had built. We toured the wood surrounding the homestead, pointing to the direction where one would locate the creek, the barn, and the barnyard. I found the site where John and Becky's three babies rested in peace. Just behind the house, they were, close enough still to be part of the family as Becky looked outside of her kitchen window. The grief I felt then was immobilizing. It defies words, so if I cannot articulate the emotions of that afternoon, it is not because I have no will to. My heart was seized violently, shaken and shattered, and given back to me, raw and torn. Three beautiful, tender infants, one girl and two boys, lay there with a goodly portion of their mother's life lying there beside them. And I could feel it all. I could not prevent the images from coming of John and Becky's struggle to keep life in those children, nor could I prevent the infusion of that despair. We left then to search out the boarding house where Charley had made residence.

How it had changed after all these years! Nonetheless, Joe and I were still able to point out its rooms. We were fortunate enough that the present inhabitants allowed us entrance. Independently, Marge asked Joe and I to point out Charley's room and, independently, we did so. Upon entering the room, I was awash in remembrance of hours spent there, some spent with ice and frost sheeting the windows, others with summer birds and breezes stirring the curtains. The memory was pleasant, oddly, since the relationship Becky and Charley shared was illicit. But it was, at the same time, a necessary one. One can only speculate now as to why, though I can say with certainty that I felt no pain in those rooms, no matter that conscience would require some.

We took to the streets once more, and again we were all breathless with the sheer adventure of it all. What a thrill it was to be here, marching right straight to locations we'd only recently discovered in a state of hypnosis. It was chilling to touch the very same earth, trees, the wood, that we had touched so long before this. It made one sense one's own smallness in this wondrous creation of a Universe, yet I was gifted with the certainty of pure invincibility from my loving God. What a precious gift this is! I thought as I thanked.

Progressing from the main street through town, past the railroad tunnel and the woods, Marge and Joe often intercepted me (in the walking trance state) as I paid no attention to pedestrian traffic rules. I would bolt headlong into the roads, with no concern for looking to the left or to the right, with no care toward vehicles wishing to share the roads with me. After a time, it became evident that I thought of myself as behaving appropriately, as I failed to hear the clip clop sound of approaching horses. I suppose these influences do run deeper than I anticipated and, fortunately, Marge was able to set that influence to rights.

All in all, we enjoyed ten highly-charged days in Millboro, filled with old sights seen through new eyes. We sailed upon rivers of nostalgia and seas of remembrance, our navigational routes taken from 100-year-old maps that have been libraried within a sleeping past. It was the best of Heaven and a taste of hell, but it had been worth it.

Finally, we trundled off in search of Becky's grave. It was Joe who first pointed it out, that tiny, iron-fenced plot at the edge of town. If the landscape had remained the same, it would have been more easily recognized, however, at our return, the fine, old church was no longer there, nor was the great barn where our village used to gather for festive occasions. Marge and Joe managed the several steps it took to reach the yard. I could not see my way clear. "What a silly I am," I told myself, but a still coldness crept over me, as if I were down there, myself . . . which I obviously was not. I remained in a frost, however, and chose not to move. Something, at that point, swept over me, and I knew what it was. It wasn't fear, as I would have supposed, since a murdered young mother lay there who was at one time me. Rather, it was sadness, a sadness that washed over me in consecutive, almost endless, waves.

What an awesome, terrible waste, I thought. A young wife and mother laid the blueprint down for the senseless destruction of so many innocent lives, and *for no point or principles whatsoever!!* There was no valor in Becky's death, no ethic set for her to be dying over, no sacrifice in the name of honor to leave a memorial to her passing. Her death, in its unvarnished truth, was the death of a tramp. I looked back on her life and death and saw the undeserved and indescribable agony inflicted upon a good man and their five innocent children. From what I had learned from Becky, I came to understand that, in many ways, Becky's John had tried desperately to save Becky's life, while she was doing her best to die. She didn't comprehend that her adulterous actions would take her down the road to the edge of town and a tiny, iron-fenced plot. I don't think John expected such an end, either.

No one really knows for certain what led to the first of Becky's affairs. Speculation and my intimate relationship with Becky left me with some very good guesses, though. Sometime after the birth of John and Becky's third or fourth surviving child, John's mother conveyed her desire to John that he let Becky in on a long-held family secret. Becky had no knowledge that John was three-quarters Indian. During that time, the Indian classes were considered to be lower in stature than the Negro. Becky had been led to believe that John was of French descent, which may have been true to a degree, as John's mother's branches of the family tree are incomplete. So, John's lack of disclosure as to the full nature of his ancestry was not actually a lie, but merely an omission. However, with his confession seemed to come a breach in Becky's trust. It seems doubtful that Becky felt John to be inferior to her, as the hypnotic feeling induced by the questions relating to Becky's reactions about it seems to indicate that she felt primarily grave hurt that John did not trust her love sufficiently to tell her the whole truth at the outset. Hindsight tells me, though, that had he disclosed this news up front, Becky's parents never would have consented to the union. Not only that, but John's Indian heritage had been a dearly guarded secret, as they and their children would have been ostracized from their community had it become public. However, Becky was not the person to confide a secret to. She often spoke miles before she considered the consequences. Her first affair began shortly after John's disclosure, and for reasons known only to Becky (if they were, indeed, known at all). It was with Samuel, who would later become the father of Becky's last-born son, the baby at her skirts in the barn. Samuel would also become my husband in this current life, Smokey Williamson.

My second trip to Millboro was a satchel of shocks, as well. October, 1992 left Marge, Smokey, and me under the same spell as Marge, Joe, and I had fallen under, and it was so wonderful again. This time, however, I was more of an observer. I was given the opportunity to eavesdrop on my husband's memories. I saw the familiar hesitation that took control at the reliving of a long ago past. I had been privy to the sights and sounds of the old town, but this was Smokey's first second look, and it was delightful, as I could feel the panorama he was experiencing, and I could taste the flavoring that seasoned his recollections. Although they were his exclusively, I remembered mine. It must have been like the way a kindergarten teacher feels when her pupils beam proudly over the first, lovely finger-painting they've done—pudgy, little fingers, still coated in rainbow colors, and broad, full grins boasting their creations. I think I can liken it to that sense of discovery and skill we experience when we achieve and observe that which we've created. This is a past that *we have* created, and we are here now to discover and appraise it.

However, there were more surprise developments in store for me, the one who had arrived in Millboro to gloat about all that I knew, having a firm grip on my supposition that there was no more I would need to learn. Wrong.

I once again had fully mapped out a range of expectations, leaving no space for alterations. However, as it turned out, very few of my expectations were fulfilled.

I had anticipated a great romantic adventure for the late Samuel and Becky, who were lovers once and who had finally married and set their record to rights. Warm, candlelit evenings were on my agenda, as were breezy, giddy walks in the new old woods. I cannot recall setting eyes on one candle there, even in a restaurant. Walking in the woods was a group venture leaving no time for romance, giddy or otherwise. They were terribly breezy, though.

What really happened was that Maureen got angry. I mean really angry. What started it was a cold bath. The Inn where we lodged had a spacious dining room, and on our second night there, they closed it up. Only invited guests were welcome, and those comprised some seventy people. We couldn't even beg a single cup of coffee. Not only that, but this entailed mountains of dishes and glassware to wash, and acre feet of hot water, plus a whole lot of time. The kitchen staff was thus busily employed before I prepared to bathe, but ignorant of this, I shook out a trendy little nighty, turned on the spouts to the bathtub, into which I had metered out several drops of lavender oil (for the complete luxury of it), brushed my teeth, and waited in the large room for the tub to fill. A few moments passed as I tied up my hair, absolutely purring in anticipation for that delicious, long, hot bath. Three-quarters full, the tub was, when I dipped a toe into it. It was then that I found out just how cold Virginia water is in late October, when it is very windy outside and the cooks have used all the hot water cleaning up.

Smokey was sprawled out on the warm bed, while I stood alone, wearing nothing but a frozen foot and a frown. I figured out what had happened the minute I recalled the private party, so I indicated to my husband that maybe he could take a stroll down the hill to check on the cooks' progress. It was *then* that I first came face to face with Samuel, who had maintained a houseful of freed slaves, as he'd called them, which in translation still meant, servants to do his bidding. Seeing that he was not real likely to tend hastily to my meager request, I threw on some sweats and sneakers and hustled down the grade to peer in through the kitchen windows. I could see the staff bustling around and overheard that they had "a hell of a lot of dishes to do." I thought another half hour should do it, but I didn't have a clear view of all the drainboards. I took back up the hill to our rooms to wait awhile. Later, finding the water still icy, I insisted that, as the man of the house, Smokey do something to salvage this night. That incited Samuel to retort that "hot water was always the responsibility of someone else to fetch for HIM!" At that point I noted that serious, immediate changes were due in this attitude, because Smokey Williamson had no slaves, nor would that status be subject to change soon.

I realized that I had met Samuel, as he was, and not as Becky had seen him. Maureen helped out there. Putting Maureen's and Becky's heads together, I realized that Becky did not have the idyllic companionship of soulmates that she had portrayed in hypnosis. This Samuel was selfish, spoiled, inconsiderate, and was in no way the gentleman that Becky (and Maureen) had perceived him to be. This gave rein to more memory, which led to a sense of "You brute!" The "peel me a grape" attitude that Smokey had adopted since touchdown in D.C. had been a direct connection to Samuel. On the whole, the trip was great, actually, but Samuel emerged on several more occasions during our stay there, and don't you think that Smokey didn't hear about it, too. I was real mad.

The hot water never was forthcoming, as the inn had blown a boiler, what with all the dishes, and we had no choice but to wait till the next day. Then, on another night during this trip, we were hit with a wicked storm. We'd been in town maybe three or four days by then, which was long enough to awaken not just the right-below-the-surface type memories, but the more subtle variety, as well.

We'd gone to bed early that night, due to the weather. It was one of those storms you could feel even through sleep. The night was pitch black, except for the brilliant shards of lightning, and it was full of sound. I could almost feel the thunder in my bones as the winds raged and howled through the attic spaces and whistled through cracks around the window frames. The rain lashed in great, solid sheets, and maybe it was that sound that caught me up into a dream of nuzzling into warm, damp hair that faintly smelled of wood smoke and pipe tobacco. I stretched again and curled into the smells, letting the storm rage unprotested outside. I was warm and safe, and the children were bundled next to and around each other in other rooms. All was perfectly well with the world . . . except for one thing; my children were all three thousand miles away from here. This was not my life, but Becky's, come to visit me that night in the storm. There was not wood smoke in our room, nor was there a pipe anyplace. I'd gotten an intimate gift that night from Becky, a loving share of her life through my memory, carried in to me on the wind and rain. I awoke pleased and smiling, even though the weather had been so unkind to us. We knew the conditions would restrict our outdoor activities if it kept up, but another gift of sunshine came later in the morning.

From my husband's point of view, knowing Samuel has helped explain a couple of odd incidents in this life. Several years ago, Smokey acquired a strange attraction to cigars—strange since firefighters normally do not smoke. He also felt silly when he impulsively bought a horse, but then actually learned how to ride it, despite his city-life roots. He stated that he occasionally got "flashes" of himself astride a horse, "as if I'd done it before." He also experienced occasional, oblique sensations of having to hide that logically had nothing to do with his present circumstances.

These incidents became much clearer for him once he had been regressed and recalled Samuel's thoughts.

While visiting Millboro, Smokey happened to stand on the porch of the general store, and he felt the most ungodly chill run through him. It was as though he'd "stood exacly there, exactly the same way, many years before." He had the strong feeling of being "caught, flat-footed, out in public where I could be spotted by anyone!" Smokey looked pasty and clearly unnerved at the sudden insight into Samuel's feelings.

When we came into Millboro, I had my hat set to do two things, if I did nothing else. First, I planned to leave flowers at the babies' graves, to remember their memories with three lovely bouquets. However, I could find no flowers for sale in Millboro, nor did I see any blooming in anybody's gardens. I was saddened, at first, but then I remembered that I hadn't forgotten to do what I came to do. I came to remember them, and that I did very well. I remembered them in life, not in death. I saw their sweet faces and felt their warm breath against my neck. I remembered to wrap their tiny, infant fingers around my heart and to look into my mind's eye, so that I could look, again, into theirs. I remembered their cuddles and their coos, as if I could ever forget. I found that I brought, instead of flowers, a mother's love that knows nobody's death, that refuses to acknowledge such a trivial event. I brought what had never been missing, and I realized, as I knelt there, clinging to the memory that never was gone and never will be, that flowers were of no conse-quence, after all.

Secondly, I came to Millboro to visit Becky's grave and to say goodbye. I thought about what I would say for three or four days before mentioning my intent to Smokey. I wanted to say goodbye, because the time had come, and it was the right thing to do, the respectful thing. I planned to say thank you for Becky's insight, for all that it had brought into my life. I had seen through her eyes and acknowledged her mistakes. I had felt her pain and loss and determined not to have them for my own. I had felt the glory of the love she had lived with, her innocence and openness, and decided to keep those. I heard her laughing, tasted her tears, and I found that I loved this woman very, very much. I had learned to understand her. I'd learned to build baby clothes from scratch, to make soap, and to stretch chickens. Becky had become my friend, a part of me that I love within myself. In the end, I never did say goodbye. How could I do so now? It was unthinkable, and it became impossible. How could I even have considered it?

I would not say goodbye to Becky, not then or now; she is here to stay, as all good friends should be. And, who knows? Maybe Becky can see now that her Elizabeth has grown into a gracious woman, after all. Baby Peter has come with his mother out of the barn, and they are both well and happy. Life has been good for Becky this time and, God willing, it will remain that way, as it should.

We may return to Millboro someday, but I doubt it will be a search and rescue mission. I think we may return simply to marvel at the landscape that is so breathtaking. To return now in order to return to the past would be defeating, since it is now time to go forward. Overviewing the past to search out its lessons had been fulfilled. I believe the major lessons of the past have been completed and here, in the present, is where I take them into my future. I hope always to be equal to the task.

CHAPTER 26

AFTERWORD

INTEREST IN PAST LIVES seems to have grown tremendously since *Mission to Millboro* was published. This is probably due in part to the fact that many medical doctors are acknowledging the benefits of past-life therapy.

My son is eminent in the field of cellular biology, and his attitude towards my work in past-life areas has, for the past several years, been one of condescending disdain. Imagine my surprise when he called me awhile back, and the conversation went something like this:

SON: "I was at a party recently and met a psychiatrist and two psychologists who are all using past-life therapy in their work, and they want to know where they can get a copy of your book."

ME: "They cannot. It won't be available for a few months."

SON: "Oh, you have a publisher. Good!"

He then proceeded to describe to me, at length and in detail, exactly how the cover should be designed. Evidently he had given it a lot of thought. The bottom line of this story is that I am happy to announce to the world that among the "Yuppie Intelligencia" of the nation, it is now considered politically correct to acknowledge past-life memories.

There are some really fine minds now studying this phenomenon. Hopefully they will not allow themselves to be limited by the perimeters of reincarnation. When searching for the truth, one must be open to all ideas and explore all avenues. Anyone in the mind-healing sciences today who subscribes to John Locke's theory of the *tabula rasa* (that the mind is a blank slate at birth), simply has not been paying attention.

As noted by Maureen, the human mind loves to "compartmentalize" all aspects of life, especially those aspects we do not fully understand. It is so easy to compartmentalize past-life experiences under the heading, "Reincarnation," because this theory offers a pat answer to all questions that arise concerning past lives.

I do not consider these past-life memories spooky or mysterious. I view these *avitas mens,* or ancient memories, as an integral part of the human being, as necessary a part of the human condition as the eyes, ears, legs, or arms.

Surely there is a valid scientific explanation as to the existence of *avitas mens* that has nothing to do with reincarnation. Our eye and hair color, body build, and other physiological make-up is determined principally by genes. What dictates which past-life memories will reside within us? Genes? I think not—too easy and too predictable. This is a mystery that may or may not eventually be answered. My opinion is that it will, and in the not too distant future. Whether or not we will ever know what triggers groups from one life to congregate together in another life is an even deeper question, and one that probably never will be rationally explained at our current levels of understanding.

Several years ago I conducted a study involving a couple of sets of identical twins and one set of identical triplets. When hypnotized, each regressed into the same past life memories as his or her sibling(s). To me, this denotes that a biological component exists in the development of the *avitas mens.* Jung felt that basic human instincts are seated in the hormones. Perhaps we must look in equally obscure areas for the roots of these memories. The result of the twin study holds true only for identicals. It was my experience that fraternal twins each have their own individual past-life memories.

This entire area is strictly theoretical. All we know for certain is that some part of the mind is always aware and recording, that we all have many past-life memories buried in our minds, and that these memories appear to be those of people who actually lived and breathed at some time in history. There is overwhelming evidence that these *avitas mens* exert a pronounced effect on our current lives.

Regarding Millboro and its surroundings, it has been called to my attention that the date on the front of Katy's tunnel is that of several years after the Civil War. When Charley described to me how they prepared the tunnel for demolition, he stated that they prepared only the first tunnel . . . he was unaware of the second. This ties in with what an elderly resident of Millboro said . . . that only the first tunnel was usable when the war started, and that the second was not built until later, during the reconstruction period after the war. The "turnaround" was built behind the first tunnel, and the spot where it stood is still highly visible. Obviously the tunnels were not dedicated and dated until both were completed.

A very well-known, famous movie star has a role in the Millboro mystery. Several people have identified him absolutely as having been there during the Civil War. A couple of them have even described his profession back then . . . and the people who did this have never been in contact with one another.

Through the years, I have watched this man on the movie screen with a dedicated fascination, an overwhelming awareness. My feelings when viewing him are inexplicable. It is as though my soul were asking, "Who *are* you?" It is a teasing, unfathomable mystery, the answer to be found deep in his eyes. Whenever he appears in a scene, for me, all others disappear. I concentrate fiercely upon him, hoping to plumb the depths of his being, to answer the mystery. Now, hopefully, the mystery is answered. The reader must understand that this is not a sexual attraction. It is very much like the sensation of knowingness I felt when first I spotted Pat Greene one evening and recognized him to be John. It is a very primal feeling that goes beyond simple recognition, perhaps like the flame to the mesmerized moth.

The reaction among the citizenry of Millboro when we exposed the buried room on Grandma's property was one of shock and disbelief. When the video camera was dropped through the ceiling hole, the cameraman connected it to a monitor so we could perceive what was being recorded. While those in the circle around the monitor gave their rapt attention to the video screen, I analyzed their faces, which were a study of incredulous skepticism. The property owner said, "Good Lord, I've driven my truck and backhoe over this room a hundred times. I'm amazed it did not cave in." Another bystander stated, "I've lived in this town all my life and so did my parents. None of us ever knew this room was down here."

After the camera crew left, the spectators dispersed, not excitedly or animatedly as one might expect, but deep in thought, some a little troubled and wondering what this meant. Everyone, even the camera crew, was strangely silent and self-absorbed.

Surely we are on the threshold of a whole new science that warrants a good deal of intelligent investigation.

LIST OF CHARACTERS

by Torrey Paulson

Torrey Paulson is one of many readers who was very impressed with Mission to Millboro *but found herself becoming confused by the myriad of characters. So she graciously undertook the job of identifying the more prominent of the group. Below are her brief descriptions of each character as they appear in alphabetical order by their first or most common name. The listings identify characters in both* Mission to Millboro *and* Return to Millboro, *giving first their past-life personality and then their present-day identity. Torrey worked as an assistant editor for a publishing house and is now a wife and mother who lives in Arvada, Colorado.* —M.R.

MISSION TO MILLBORO

AVA WAVERLY: She was Constance's mother. She often acted strangely, and townspeople thought she was a little crazy, but she may have been drugged by her husband to hide her suspicions of his black magic activities. She was stunningly beautiful and rich, but very unhappy. After her husband died, she burned down the family home.

> CURRENT IDENTITY NOT REVEALED: This woman is called "Alice" but that is not her real name. She is a current-day friend of both Maureen (Becky) and "Nancy" (Constance).

BECKY'S CHILDREN: PHOEBE/PHEBE, ROBERT, RACHEL, ELIZABETH, and BABY PETER ASHFORD (AILSTOCK/AUSHLICK): They were the five surviving children in John and Becky's family, out of the eight children Becky had. (Baby Peter was actually fathered by Samuel, the printer/spy). ELIZABETH married John Thacker in 1868. He ran the town feed store. They had children together, but she died fairly young. More about BABY PETER is listed under the characters of *Return to Millboro*.

DIANA LOVEGREN: She worked in Lake Elsinore City Hall for several years. She has lived in the Lake Elsinore area for about fifteen years.

CHAD: He was one of the Union spy ring in Virginia. Samuel's newspaper was full of secret messages and geared toward operatives like Chad. CURRENT IDENTITY UNKNOWN.

CHARLEY MORGAN: This man was born as Charles Patterson. He became a secret Confederate sympathizer/agent. His cover was as a civilian horse trainer in Millboro named "Charley Morgan." While in Millboro, Charley fell in love with Becky and became her long-term lover. He became friends with her children as well.

As Charles Patterson, he had graduated early from West Point and was commissioned into the Union Army. Soon afterward, however, he joined the Confederacy, was wounded early in the war, and was then sent undercover to Millboro as a spy. His secret mission was to blow up the railroad tunnel, and massive amounts of stockpiled army supplies, if the Union forces ever threatened to take the town. Charley had a hard time coping with Becky's death, so after leaving Millboro, he drifted. Finally, in Georgia, he died at a relatively young age, after sustaining a head wound in a saloon brawl.

JOE NAZAROWSKI: Joe, a Lake Elsinore man, has had an extensive background in law enforcement. He served in the U.S. Army in 1964-1967 in Vietnam and in the Marine Corps from 1970-1972. About six months after the study began, Joe (recalling his life as Charley) was able to locate many significant spots in Millboro during a trip to that location, including where Charley's horse corral had stood and the corner room in the boarding house where he had lived (and where Becky would sneak in to visit him). Joe also was able to show study participants the holes he (as Charley) drilled in the railroad tunnel walls outside Millboro, ready for explosive gunpowder charges, in case the Union forces threatened to take the tunnel and stockpiled supplies around town. Joe also remembered where Becky had been buried in an unmarked grave and was able to identify the location to stunned study participants.

CONSTANCE WAVERLY: She was the daughter of a Millboro town official. She was rich, spoiled, and could be a venomous little snip at times. Although she pretended to be a friend to Becky, Constance would have affairs and tell the men involved that she was Becky and that her husband was the town lawman. The inevitable gossip around town tarnished Becky's reputation even further. Constance had her own designs on Samuel, so she threatened him with exposure, thereby forcing him to give up his affair with Becky. Constance's father forced her to marry a man named Garrett, a political crony of his.

> CURRENT IDENTITY NOT REVEALED: This woman was called "Nancy" to protect her identity, but that is not her real name. She lives in a town near Lake Elsinore and knows Maureen (Becky). Constance had flaming red hair and so does "Nancy" today.

ELIZABETH: Youngest daughter of Becky and John. Elizabeth was hiding in the hay loft of the barn and witnessed her mother's murder.

> DIANE LOVEGREN: an Elsinore matron.

HOPPY HARPER: He was a part-time fur trader and gambling partner who did odd jobs for Honey's first husband, Thomas Mason. Hoppy was so dirty and smelly that he wasn't allowed to go inside during a large, festive Millboro party.

> CURRENT IDENTITY UNKNOWN.

JAKE BAUER: He was a nasty, ne'er-do-well, stealing drunk and drifter, who murdered Becky on orders of Union spies. He also did odd jobs for the Confederacy. He had clashed earlier with John (Becky's husband) over stolen sheep and cows which Jake had stolen from John's neighbor and then attempted to sell. After Becky's murder, Jake was ambushed and hung by John, Charley, and John's cousin, Jeff.

> CURRENT IDENTITY UNKNOWN.

KATY: She was the Millboro town prostitute working on her own, for whom "Katy's Tunnel" was named. She was a friend of John.

> CURRENT IDENTITY UNKNOWN.

LILA: She was a close friend to Elizabeth. Lila's father was Jeff, John's younger cousin.

JAN DUNWOODY: She lives in Elsinore and owns her own beauty shop. She is a long-time friend of the author, Marge Rieder. She worked in an office near to that of Joe Nazarowski and always felt a tangle of negative emotions every time she saw him, yet she didn't know him and had never even talked to him. In regression sessions she remembered herself as Lila seeing Charley (Joe) being mean to his horses at the Millboro corral in the middle of town, something many study participants also had recalled.

LITTLE EAGLE (or WHITE EAGLE): He was a revered Indian man who resided in Robin's Nest, the son of the "wise one." He married Liz (renamed Singing Bird by the Indians at Robin's Nest) in an Indian ceremony and later became the father of "Pony Boy," who grew up to be John, Becky's husband and the lawman in Millboro. During the war, John headed up the Union spy ring in the Millboro area, at his father's prompting. Little Eagle felt resentful that his wife, Singing Bird, and son, Pony Boy, had been forced by the tribal council to live in Millboro so Pony Boy could get a good education. Little Eagle resented that Pony Boy was being turned into a white man. As a result, when Little Eagle learned of an abandoned white boy (later known as White Bear), he taught that lad Indian hunting and survival skills, in effect, turning the boy into an Indian. Little Eagle helped keep White Bear alive. When the government forced the Robin's Nest Indians to relocate onto a reservation, Little Eagle and other braves took refuge in the woods to avoid that fate.

CURRENT IDENTITY UNKNOWN.

LIZ or SINGING BIRD: Singing Bird was born about 1815 in an Indian village in Virginia, the daughter of a white man, Frank Gillian, and an Indian woman named Winja, or Raining Eyes. After the death of her first husband, Jud Ailstock, Singing Bird married Little Eagle/White Eagle, and they lived in the Robin's Nest Indian camp above Millboro. They had a son, Pony Boy, who later became known as John Daniel Ashford (Ailstock/Aushlick). As Pony Boy got bigger, the tribal council forced Singing Bird and Pony Boy to live in Millboro, passing as whites, so the boy could get a good education. Little Eagle secretly visited Liz when he could. After he told her about his helping the abandoned boy, White Bear, Liz began regularly baking loaves of bread for Little Eagle to take to him, along with other food. This comforting help from Liz during his constant struggle for survival made a big impression on White Bear, and came up in a very touching way as told in *Mission to Millboro*.

BARBARA ROBERTS is now deceased.

MARY: Mary had a very deep friendship with Liz, and they were neighbors in Millboro, where Mary owned a horse farm. Mary always kept the secret that Liz was married to Little Eagle. Mary's husband was Steven. After he went away to the Civil War, she lost their house and land to bad people during the war. She went up to Baltimore and worked as an accountant, always trying to save enough money to regain her land in the Millboro area. Her story is told in detail in *Mission to Millboro*.

LINDA ROBERTS ROSS: Linda is the oldest daughter of Barbara Roberts (Liz). Linda is the part owner/manager of a business in Norwalk, California, and she lives about an hour's drive from Lake Elsinore. Regression sessions revealed that the best friends who knew everything about each other back in Millboro (Liz and Mary), became a mother and daughter in today's current lifetime.

PHILIP TAYLOR: Honey knew this man before she married Thomas Mason, and always said that she should have married Philip instead. After Thomas was killed for cheating in a card game and the war ended, she did marry Philip. He was a Union soldier. Following the war, Philip, Honey, baby Peter, and others eventually left Millboro for the Richmond area.

CURRENT IDENTITY UNKNOWN.

ROSE: Rose was a "fancy lady" who ran the bawdy house at Millboro's edge of town. She became John's lover as part of his spy activities. Her bawdy house helped pass on war information to the Union side via John.

CURRENT IDENTITY UNKNOWN.

RUNNING BEAR: He was Ruthie's Indian lover and the father of her baby daughter. He was a good man, and Ruthie loved him desperately.

CURRENT IDENTITY UNKNOWN.

SARAH (possibly SARAH JEAN CASHMAN): She was a young New England nurse volunteer sent to Millboro to fight the raging epidemic which had been killing people by the hundreds. The disease was believed to have been typhoid, caused by the contaminated food and water people throughout the South had been exposed to during the last several months of the war. Although she had planned to immediately marry after the War's end and get her life back on course, she couldn't ignore the desperate situation. As a result, she volunteered to lead about twenty people, mostly nurses with a few doctors, in the Millboro epidemic relief effort. Later, after the epidemic ended, Sarah returned up North, married, and had two children. She died in 1891

MARGE RIEDER, PH.D.: She is the author of *Mission to Millboro* and *Return to Millboro*, as well as the primary hypnotist in the group past-life study. Several study participants identified her as having participated in the Millboro saga, and under hypnotic regression, she recalled the life of Sarah. More complete information about her current life work in experimental hypnosis and past-life regression appears in *Mission to Millboro*.

THOMAS MASON: He was Honey's first husband. He won the Millboro boarding house by gambling but was later shot and killed for cheating at cards.
CURRENT IDENTITY UNKNOWN.

WARM SUN: A squaw who lived in Robin's Nest when Liz (Singing Bird did. They became friends.
ROBIN PARK: Now deceased.

WHITE BEAR: He was a small white boy who was abandoned by his aunt during wagon-train repairs outside the Indian encampment above Millboro. He slept at night under town buildings and scrounged for food until a saloon-keeper took pity on him and gave him food and a place to sleep in exchange for chores. Later, Little Eagle helped the boy dig a cave into the mountain above Millboro and taught him how to fish and catch small game. In an effort to protect the boy, Little Eagle told the Indian tribe that the boy was crazy, so the Indians and townspeople all gave him wide berth for many years and let him live in peace. He was named "White Bear," because he was white and lived in a cave.

White Bear secretly fell deeply in love with Becky. He used Indian medical techniques to help heal Becky's sick cow, but other than that, the contact between White Bear and Becky was only sporadic. Becky avoided him, because, like everyone else, she thought the man was crazy. As a result, he never got a chance to express his feelings toward her before she was killed. Later, White Bear felt intense guilt, since he had seen Becky's killer near her home and could have stopped the murder if he had only known what was about to happen. Years later, he still had a hard time dealing with his grief, so one day, White Bear just decided to die alone on the top of his mountain. His fascinating, touching story is given in full in *Mission to Millboro*.

DAVE GREMLING: Dave served in the U.S. Army in Vietnam. At the time of the study, he had lived in Lake Elsinore for twelve years. He is the father of Luke Gremling (Baby Peter).

RETURN TO MILLBORO

ALICE ("ALLIE") possibly MORGAN or JOHNSON: She was a young girl whose family was deeply involved in Millboro's Underground Railroad activities. She had a younger sister and brother. Her mother's name may have been "Jane." Sally and Allie were childhood friends.

TERRY POMPA: She is the mother of two children, and she is a student. She lived in Lake Elsinore about eight years but currently lives in Las Vegas, Nevada. She has never been to Virginia. She is a friend of Jo Collier.

ANDREW A. and MARY JANE AILSTOCK: This couple married in Millboro and later had a son, Payton R. Ailstock. Becky's public reaction to the marriage created long-term problems for her own marriage. Becky mistakenly believed that Andrew was John's cousin. She objected during the marriage ceremony because the bride and groom were closely related, and she felt the marriage tarnished the Ailstock name. (John hadn't told Becky yet that he was three-quarters Indian, and that the Ailstocks were no blood relation to him.) When Becky later found out the truth from John about his own background, she was upset because she felt John was of a lower social class and that their children were illegitimate, since marriages between whites and Indians were not allowed under the law at the time. Becky's negative reaction to this revelation began to unravel her rock-solid marriage and prompted her to begin a string of retaliatory affairs which eventually indirectly led to her death.

CURRENT IDENTITIES UNKNOWN.

BABY PETER—PETER ASHFORD: He was Becky's youngest son. His father was Samuel, the printer/spy. After his mother, Becky, was murdered, he was sent to live with Honey, who ran the Millboro boarding house. Many years later, he ran away to join the Texas Rangers. During his travels, he briefly met John, Becky's former husband, by chance in the Indian territory (now Oklahoma). At age 42, Peter married a woman named Becky in Arizona, and they had three children together. He retired from the Rangers, and they went back to Millboro, Virginia, to research his mother's murder, but everyone who knew anything had passed on or left the area. Peter was killed at age 64 in New Mexico, when he was shot by a man whom he had jailed earlier.

LUKE GREMLING: Luke was born in Orange, California. He is the youngest son of Maureen (Becky) and Dave Gremling (White Bear). Luke is a young firefighter, and he also attends college. He has lived in the Elsinore area for eighteen years and has never been to Virginia.

BECKY—REBECCA CUNNINGHAM: Becky was the central character in *Mission to Millboro*. She married John Daniel Ashford (Ailstock/Aushlick), who became the Millboro marshal. She was born ca. 1835 in Herndon, Virginia, daughter of a blacksmith. While married to John, Becky began an affair with a Confederate secret agent posing as a civilian horse trainer, known locally as "Charley Morgan." Their long, torrid affair eventually indirectly led to her death. She also had an affair with Samuel Phaelan (or Pelter), and he fathered her last child, baby Peter. Five of Becky's eight children survived. They were Robert, Rachel, Elizabeth, Phoebe, and baby Peter.

MAUREEN WILLIAMSON: Maureen was born in Boston, Massachusetts, and has lived in the Elsinore, California area for eighteen years. She is the mother of four children and is currently occupied as a homemaker, busy raising her young daughter. Maureen's latent, fascinating memories of Becky's life triggered the discovery of the entire Millboro saga. Before research on this story began, she had never been to Virginia, but she has been to Millboro twice since then to investigate remembered sites. In this life, Maureen married two men who believe they knew Becky in their Millboro lives. One was Dave Gremling (White Bear), whose story is told in *Mission to Millboro*. The other is Ralph "Smokey" Williamson (Samuel), Becky's current husband. Becky remains friends with Joe Nazarowski, the man believed to be the former Charley Morgan. She first met Pat Greene (the man who believes he was formerly John Daniel Ashford, Becky's husband) after publication of *Mission to Millboro*.

CHARLEY MORGAN, aka PATTERSON: Wounded Confederate officer who came to Millboro early in the war, ostensibly to train horses. His real mission was to blow up the tunnel should Yanks invade the town. Became involved in a romance with Becky.

JOE NAZAROWSKI: Currently lives near Ontario, California and is employed as a security guard.

COFFEE: He was a young Negro boy who drowned while trying to help John and Samuel rescue Yankee soldiers trapped underneath Bratton's Bridge. Coffee had suggested that the group attach blankets to their shoes to muffle the sounds of their progress along the railroad tracks. However, John and Samuel didn't know that Coffee couldn't swim or even tread water, and the heavy blankets pulled Coffee under the water.

CURRENT IDENTITY UNKNOWN.

ELIZABETH of Green Valley Farm: She lived with and assisted an old man in running the plantation house in Green Valley, after Ruthie had left for the bawdy house. (His name may have been Colonel or Captain Lewis.) Elizabeth and he helped escaped slaves, and lost or escaped Union soldiers, by Underground Railroad activities. Previously, Elizabeth had a boy and a girl by her first husband, a Confederate war hero who died. She didn't know that her second husband had always coveted his own brother's wife and that he still loved that brother's wife. As a result, a scandal broke out during the Civil War when her second husband located his brother's wife, falsely told her that her husband (his brother) had been killed in the war, and then finessed her into going to bed with him. The brother hadn't died, so, in a twist of fate, he found his wife and brother in bed together and, as a result, shot and killed them both. Since the slain man was Elizabeth's second husband, that left her a widow again. Because both families feared the scandal could ruin the children, Elizabeth's children were taken away by the Confederate war hero's relatives to raise, and Elizabeth was sent to help the old man at Green Valley Farm, near Millboro. After the war ended, Elizabeth left the plantation.

SHARON OLIVE: Sharon was born in Minnesota, and she currently lives in Texas. She is divorced and has two children and one grandchild. She has never been to Virginia and had never heard of Millboro until this study got underway.

FELIX (PHAELAN or PELTER): He was the brother of Samuel, his only living relative at the time. Felix wanted nothing to do with running their parents' plantation, so he let Samuel do it. Felix married Carolyn of Millboro, acquired a lot of land and raised horses. Samuel lived in fear that Felix would discover Samuel's affair with Becky.

CURRENT IDENTITY UNKNOWN.

"GRANDMA" BERTHA ("BERTIE") CULLINS or COLLINS: She and her husband helped with Underground Railroad activities in hidden rooms and tunnels under their house and shed in old Millboro. Bertie was raising her granddaughter, Sally, who had been orphaned as a baby.

CURRENT IDENTITY UNKNOWN.

HONEY: She hated her real name, Marie Elizabeth, so everyone called her "Honey." She was a popular, charming woman who owned and operated Millboro's boarding house. As part of the Underground Railroad activities, Honey brought all the food left over from her boarding house restaurant every night, out to "Grandma's" home to feed the Negroes and Union soldiers hidden in secret underground rooms. She had been unhappily married to a gambler, Thomas Mason. He won the large boarding house in Millboro through gambling, but he was killed later when caught cheating in a card game. Honey and Thomas had two girls, Martha and Marie, both of whom died young. After the Civil War, Honey married her former love, a Union soldier named Philip Taylor, and she, Philip, some other relatives, and baby Peter (Becky's child) all moved away from Millboro.

> MILLIE SPROUSE: Millie was born in Alabama. She lives in Lake Elsinore and has never been to Virginia. She is an office manager in a family business. She is the mother of two daughters.

JIM TAYLOR: This is the possible name of the doctor in the Indian territory who tried unsuccessfully to heal John's cut and infected leg wound.

CURRENT IDENTITY UNKNOWN.

JOHN DANIEL ASHFORD (AILSTOCK/AUSHLICK): John was Becky's husband. He was the son of Little Eagle and Liz (Singing Bird) of Robin's Nest and was known as Pony Boy as a child. When he was a young boy, the tribal council forced Liz to take him to live in Millboro, passing as whites, so Pony Boy (John) could get a good education, hopefully to return someday to teach the youth of the tribe. John became the town marshal in Millboro. He was also the head of an extensive Union spy ring based in Millboro and covertly assisted people working in the Underground Railroad. Following his marriage to Becky, and the beginning of the Civil War, John became friends with Charley, Becky's secret lover. Charley was working as a Confederate agent sent undercover to Millboro. After Becky was killed, John placed the children in good Millboro homes, and eventually joined the Oglala, his father's tribe, out west. John was a leader who advocated negotiating with the white man, instead of running or fighting. After settling his splinter group of Indian followers outside a small town in the Indian territory (now Oklahoma), John became the town's marshal in an effort to further protect his Indian followers. At one point, baby Peter, now grown up, ran into him there by chance and visited briefly. Five years after settling the Indians outside the town, John died, at about age 45, as the result of tetanus contracted from a farming accident. He had always felt an overwhelming sadness after the Millboro years ended.

PAT GREENE: Pat was born in Downey, California. He has lived in Lake Elsinore for eleven years. Pat is a professional sheet metal worker, and he also works as a musician and entertainer. Until recently, he had never been to Virginia. Study participants generally agree that Pat Greene more closely resembles his Millboro counterpart, John Daniel Ashford, than anyone else involved in this saga. His personality today is that of John's—affable and very likable, intense, dedicated, close-mouthed, excellent sense of humor, extremely stubborn, and thoroughly involved in any cause he supports. His appearance, right down to the burning green eyes, is almost identical to John's. Several study participants who didn't know Pat, were stunned when they first met him, because they immediately and spontaneously recognized him to be the former John.

MISS KATE: She ran the boarding house in the Indian territory (which later became Oklahoma) where John worked as the town lawman.
CURRENT IDENTITY UNKNOWN.

MR. (COLONEL) LEWIS and his WIFE: They were an older couple who had a house on the Green Valley Farm. They were heavily involved in the Underground Railroad activities.
CURRENT IDENTITIES UNKNOWN.

LIZ, aka SINGING BIRD: Born to an Indian mother and an Irish father. She married an Ailstock and moved to the Millboro area. Upon his death, she married Little Eagle, an Indian from Robin's Nest. Their only son, John, later became a lawman in Millboro and married Becky.

BARBARA ROBERTS: Now deceased.

LOCK BONGA (or SUNFLOWER): She was a girl of Soaring Eagle's tribe who had been chosen by tribal elders as his intended bride.

CURRENT IDENTITY UNKNOWN.

MARTHA (possibly HEATH or HARRIS) FARMER: She was the adored wife of Roy Farmer. Before her marriage, Martha's family had moved to Virginia from Pittsburgh, Pennsylvania. She married Roy Farmer about Sept. 5, 1819, in Virginia (probably in Williamsville). Together they had four children: Matthew, Adam, Samuel, and baby Eve. Adam and Samuel worked the farm, and Matthew became a highly-paid lawyer up North.

> LYNN FARMER: Lynn is Evie Rieder's current roommate. She was born in Los Angeles, California, and raised in Gardena, California. She is an engineering services administrator. Until recently, she had never been to Virginia.

MARY ALICE WILSON: She was the wife of Henry Wilson, the Millboro undertaker. Henry called her "Alice" because his mother's name was "Mary."

> JO COLLIER: Jo is a native of California, and she's lived in Lake Elsinore for ten years. She is a former city employee of Lake Elsinore. She now works in a finance-related field. She has driven through Virginia once and stopped briefly in Norfolk.

PAUL RIDGEWAY: He may have been instrumental in making arrangements to shelter the lost Yankee soldiers in a secret room under the Cauthorn house near Millboro, after John and Samuel had rescued the men from underneath Bratton's Bridge.

CURRENT IDENTITY UNKNOWN.

ROY FARMER: He was a dairy farmer who lived outside of Williamsville, Virginia, about ten miles north of Millboro. Roy was an uneducated immigrant who came alone to America from Ireland at age 22. He courted Martha for about six months before they eloped, and they had a good life together. Roy died just prior to the advent of the Civil War.

EVIE RIEDER: Evie is the daughter of author Marge Rieder. Evie had long insisted that she was involved in the Millboro saga. Regression sessions upheld her conviction. Evie recalled two Millboro area lifetimes. The first was as Running Springs, a Robin's Nest Indian woman and spirit guardian to her people's artifacts and burial ground. She remembered her next lifetime as that of Roy Farmer.

RUNNING SPRINGS (or SPRINGS): She lived for many years in the Robin's Nest area. Her father once had been chief, but since both her parents died when she was small, she was raised by the tribe. When she was a young teenager, she had a lover, Soaring Eagle (Eagle or Eagle Boy), whom she deeply loved. Even after his death, she remained true to him for the rest of her life. She never married but looked after tribal children. She had special skills useful to the tribe. She believes that a part of her spirit remains near the white rock of the Robin's Nest Indian burial ground. She claimed "that her spirit lived on long after her death, and that she was aware of all that had transpired since her demise." Some believe her spirit has been channelled repeatedly throughout the centuries in an effort to enlighten the white man about her tribe's culture and to guard the sacred kivas.

EVIE RIEDER: Evie was born in Miami, Florida, and until recently has never been to Millboro, Virginia. She is a tool-maker and daughter of author Marge Rieder. Under regression, Evie recalled two Millboro lifetimes: one as Running Springs, an Indian girl living in the Robin's Nest area above Millboro, and a later one as Roy Farmer, who operated a dairy farm near Millboro. Evie was the first person in the Millboro regression study group to regress to a life as a member of the opposite sex.

RUTHIE: After her parents were killed, she was sent to live with her Aunt Ava and Cousin Constance Waverly's family. Because Ruthie was pretty, Constance was very envious and made Ruthie's life miserable. As a result of the problems, she was then sent to the Green Valley Farm plantation, where an older couple adopted her. Sometime later, she began to live and work at Rose's bawdy house in Millboro. Much of Ruthie's touching story is told in *Mission to Millboro*. She had a secret lover, an Indian man named Running Bear, whom she loved desperately. When she had a baby girl by him, the Indians at Robin's Nest cared for the baby. Ruthie was devastated when she watched helplessly as her young daughter was relocated with the tribe to a reservation years later. Ruthie was killed at age 32, victim of a random accident in the bawdy house.

JACKIE SPAGNOLO: Jackie is a long-time friend of Maureen. She worked for many years at Disneyland in Anaheim, California, but is now retired. She was born in Winchester, Virginia. She has lived in the Elsinore, California area for twelve years. After coming out of hypnotic regression in which she talked about loving Running Bear, she was flabbergasted. She realized that she had painted a portrait of Running Bear years before during an art class, and that the painting bore an uncanny resemblance to the man she remembered. "This is my man," she had thought during the painting session. The portrait had hung on a wall in her home for years before she hypnotically regressed to that memory.

SALLY: She was a young, sickly girl in Millboro during the Civil War. Her parents died when she was a baby, and she was raised by her grandmother, Bertha ("Bertie") Cullins or Collins. Sally helped "Grandma" hide Negroes and Union soldiers in hidden rooms under the house. Sally had a powerful crush on Charley Morgan (today's Joe Nazarowski) and would watch him at the corral. Sally died at age thirteen from small pox.

LENETTE BRYCHEL: Lenette was born in Chicago, Illinois, and now lives in Las Vegas, Nevada. She is a property auditor inspector and professional psychic. She has visited Lake Elsinore twice. Until recently, she had never been to Virginia. She is a long-time friend of Joe Nazaroski's (Charley Morgan).

SAM BROWN, REV.: He was the Windy Cove Presbyterian Church minister who married Andrew A. and Mary Jane Ailstock in Millboro. When Becky raised objections to the marriage ceremony, she and the pastor got into a big public scene.
CURRENT IDENTITY UNKNOWN.

SAMUEL PHAELAN (or PELTER): Samuel was raised in Roanoke, Virginia. After his parents' death, he moved into their plantation house between Warm Springs and Millboro and oversaw its operation. When the War broke out, John talked him into joining the Union spy ring. He opened a small printing shop and started publishing a sporadic newsletter called the "Pen and Quill," which he mailed out of Millboro. The print shop and newsletter served as a cover for his spying activities. Samuel helped filch

Confederate war supplies, especially rifles and blankets, and would take the haul to a place where items were stored until they could be smuggled up North. He also bought booze cheaply from local stills and sold it at outrageous profit to Confederate troops. Samuel and Becky had a short affair which ended abruptly with Becky pregnant with baby Peter. Constance, who had her own eye on Samuel, had forced Samuel to give up Becky by threatening to tell Samuel's sickly, vindictive wife about the affair. Becky never knew why Samuel broke it off. Becky was always in his heart, and the situation was very painful. He carried a torch for her the rest of his life.

RALPH "SMOKEY" WILLIAMSON: Ralph was born in Michigan. He works as a firefighter. Ralph has lived in the Elsinore area for twenty-five years. He has visited Millboro once, following publication of *Mission to Millboro*. Ralph is married to Maureen (Becky).

SNOWBIRD: She was an Indian girl who had been orphaned as a child, so she lived with her aunt, uncle, and three boy cousins. She learned about healing with medicinal herbs from her aunt. Snowbird died suddenly from a fever at about age sixteen.

CASSIE: Cassie lives in Temecula, California. For privacy reasons, she asked not to be further identified.

SOARING EAGLE (or EAGLE BOY or EAGLE): He was a young brave, the chief's eldest son, who lived among the Indians of Robin's Nest in the 1600s. He loved Running Springs, a girl from a different but related tribe, and they met secretly at dusk numerous times before his untimely death. He was killed as a young brave in battle when his hunting party was ambushed by a hostile tribe.

JOANN KELLEY: Joann was born in Murphy, North Carolina, and is a graduate of the University of Western North Carolina. She has lived in California since 1964. She is a teacher of elementary education and a language arts specialist. She has never been to Millboro.

STELLA: She would pick up four-year-old John at Liz's Millboro home, put him into a wagon, and take him to school. She may have been the school teacher.

CURRENT IDENTITY UNKNOWN.

SUE: She was John's occasional companion in the small town in the Indian territory out West. Sue was a pretty, friendly, working girl.

CURRENT IDENTITY UNKNOWN.

TOWNLEY CAUTHORN: He married Martha Bratton and opened a high-class general store in Millboro. He built and owned the house which sheltered the Yankee soldiers whom John and Samuel had rescued earlier from underneath Bratton's Bridge. A small, privy-like shack on his property hid a below-ground room used in Underground Railroad activities.

CURRENT IDENTITY UNKNOWN.

MR. WARREN: He ran the big general store in Millboro. He talked pro-Union politics and stirred up trouble, but secretly supported the Confederacy.

CURRENT IDENTITY UNKNOWN.

WHITE STAR: When she was a young girl, her Indian family came from up North to the Robin's Nest area to hide from white men. Her mother died when she was young, so she and her older brother were raised by their father (as in Kathi's life today). White Star married Dancing Bear, and they had three children. She died at age 27 from a chest ailment, shortly before the Indians were forced out of Robin's Nest.

KATHI SHANNON: Kathi was born in Redwood City, California, and has never been to Virginia. Kathi has worked as a barber and is currently training to be a hypnotherapist. She is currently living in Lake Elsinore and is married with one son.

WILL—WILLIAM O. WINSTON, JR.: He was a tall, smart West Point student who became part of the Confederate spy ring in Western Virginia. When he was an undercover spy, he was called "Mr. Hobbs."

Will's mother was a Northerner whose maiden name may have been Anderson. His father was a regular Army officer from the deep South and a West Point graduate. Will had an older brother, Steven, and a younger sister, Cynthia. When Will was young, his mother and sister were murdered in an Indian massacre in a remote, wooded area, possibly in Wisconsin, while Will, his brother, and other men were on a hunting trip. Will blamed his father for leaving his family in a vulnerable location rather than letting them stay at a well-protected military fort. Will was filled with hatred and bitterness toward his father because of this for the rest of his life.

Later, Will entered West Point, where he met Charles Patterson, the man later known as "Charley Morgan." Charles recognized that Will, too, had secret Confederate sympathies and "chewed his butt" to make sure Will became an excellent officer. Eventually Will became a secret Confederate operative, just like Charley. After the war, Will just let his father and paternal relatives think he was dead. Eventually he went to California to live.

LYNE BOCK: Lyne is a California native and a student. She has lived in Lake Elsinore since 1978. She has never been to Virginia.

CURRENT DAY PEOPLE WHO HAVE ASSISTED AUTHOR MARGE RIEDER

LARRY FRESH: He is a Millboro realtor who owns the big house which Will recalled raiding when he was looking for John, a hidden room, and any evidence of Underground Railroad activities.

HARRY JOLLY: He lives in Burlington, North Carolina. His mother was a Bratton, and he was born and raised in the old house above Bratton's Bridge. It is Harry who supplied us with information regarding the railroad spur near Bratton's Bridge. He is related by marriage to Anna Cauthorn and was able to furnish us with information about the old Cauthorn house.

ABOUT THE AUTHOR

MARGE RIEDER has worked in the field of experimental hypnosis for more than twenty years. She has lectured throughout southern California on Past-Life Regression and conducted classes on Visual Imagery and Self-Hypnosis.

After attending Santa Ana College, she received advanced degrees from Newport University in Hypnosis and Behavior Modification. She is a graduate of the Professional Hypnosis Center in Tustin, California, is registered with the Hypnotists Examining Council, and is a member of the American Guild of Hypnotherapists, the American Board of Hypnotherapy, and the Association for Past Life Research and Therapies. She has published a number of articles in magazines and professional journals.

Currently Marge is living in Hemet, California, where she continues her study of the past-life phenomenon.

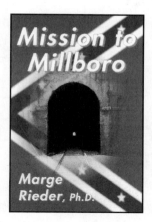